Opening Moves

Bedford Way Papers

ISSN 0261—0078

1. 'Fifteen Thousand Hours': A Discussion
Barbara Tizard et al.
ISBN 0 85473 090 7

2. The Government in the Classroom
J Myron Atkin
ISBN 0 85473 089 3

3. Issues in Music Education
Charles Plummeridge et al.
ISBN 0 85473 105 9

4. No Minister: A Critique of the D E S Paper 'The School Curriculum'
John White et al.
ISBN 0 85473 115 6

5. Publishing School Examination Results: A Discussion
Ian Plewis et al.
ISBN 0 85473 116 4

6. Work and Women: A Review
Janet Holland
ISBN 0 85473 119 9

8. Girls and Mathematics: The Early Years
Rosie Walden and Valerie Walkerdine
ISBN 0 85473 124 5

9. Reorganisation of Secondary Education in Manchester
Dudley Fiske
ISBN 0 85473 125 3

10. How Many Teachers? Issues of Policy, Planning and Demography
Tessa Blackstone and Alan Crispin
ISBN 0 85473 133 4

11. The Language Monitors
Harold Rosen
ISBN 0 85473 134 2

12. Meeting Special Educational Needs: The 1981 Act and its Implications
John Welton et al.
ISBN 0 85473 136 9

13. Geography in Education Now
Norman Graves et al.
ISBN 0 85473 219 5

14. Art Education: Heritage and Prospect
Anthony Dyson et al.
ISBN 0 85473 149 0

15. Is Teaching a Profession?
Peter Gordon (ed.)
ISBN 0 85473 220 9

16. Teaching Political Literacy
Alex Porter (ed.)
ISBN 0 85473 154 7

17. Opening Moves: Study of Children's Language Development
Margaret Meek (ed.)
ISBN 0 85473 161 X

18. Secondary School Examinations
Jo Mortimore and Peter Mortimore
ISBN 0 85473 167 9

19. Lessons Before Midnight: Educating for Reason in Nuclear Matters
The Bishop of Salisbury, et al
ISBN 0 85473 189 X

20. Education plc?: Headteachers and the New Training Initiative
Janet Maw et al
ISBN 0 85473 191 1

21. The Tightening Grip: Growth of Central Control of the School Curriculum
Denis Lawton
ISBN 0 85473 201 2

22. The Quality Controllers: A Critique of the White Paper 'Teaching Quality'
Frances Slater (ed.)
ISBN 0 85473 212 8

23. Education: Time for a New Act?
Richard Aldrich and Patricia Leighton
ISBN 0 85473 217 9

24. Girls and Mathematics: from Primary to Secondary Schooling
Rosie Walden and Valerie Walkerdine
ISBN 0 85473 222 5

25. Psychology and Schooling: What's the Matter?
Guy Claxton et al.
ISBN 0 85473 228 4

First published in 1983 by the Institute of Education, University of London,
20 Bedford Way, London WC1H 0AL. Reprinted 1985.

Distributed by Turnaround Distribution Ltd., 27 Horsell Road,
London N5 1XL (telephone: 01-609 7836).

First published in the United States 1985, Heinemann Educational Books Inc.,
70 Court Street, Portsmouth, New Hampshire 03801.

United States ISBN 0 435 08250 7 (U.S.)

Cover design by Herb Gillman

The opinions expressed in these papers are those of the authors and do not necessarily reflect those of the publisher.

© Institute of Education, University of London, 1985
All rights reserved.

ISBN 0 85473 161 X

British Library Cataloguing in Publication Data

Opening moves: work in progress in the study of children's language development. —
    (Bedford Way papers, ISSN 0261-0078; 17)
    1. Children — Language
    I. Meek, Margaret, *1925* — II. Series
    401'.9   LB1139.L3

ISBN 0-85473-161-X
ISBN 0-435-08250-7 (U.S.)

Printed in Great Britain by Reprographic Services
Institute of Education, University of London.

Opening Moves

Work in Progress in the Study of Children's Language Development

Margaret Meek (editor), Carol Fox, Henrietta Dombey, Marian Whitehead, Colin Walter, Barry Stierer

Bedford Way Papers 17
Institute of Education, University of London
distributed by Turnaround Distribution Ltd.

Contents

Introduction: Ways of looking
Margaret Meek   7

1. Talking Like a Book: Young children's oral monologues
   Carol Fox   12

2. Learning the Language of Books
   Henrietta Dombey   26

3. Proto-narrative Moves in Early Conversations
   Marian Whitehead   44

4. Form or Formula? The practice of poetry teaching
   Colin Walter   56

5. A Researcher Reading Teachers Reading Children Reading; making sense of reading assessment in the classroom
   Barry Stierer   72

Note on Authors

Carol Fox is currently engaged in a research project 'language in the nursery school' at the Newcastle-upon-Tyne Polytechnic. She has taught for many years in London comprehensive schools.

Henrietta Dombey is Senior Lecturer in the Primary Education Department of Brighton Polytechnic. She is chiefly concerned with the teaching of reading.

Marian Whitehead is Senior Lecturer in the School of Education at Goldsmiths' College, University of London. She is chiefly concerned there with the preparation of teachers for work in infant schools and in children's language development.

Colin Walter is Senior Lecturer in the School of Education at Goldsmiths' College, University of London. He has previously taught in junior and secondary schools and has worked in special education.

Barry Stierer is Research Officer for the Parental Help with Reading in Schools Project at the University of London Institute of Education.

All these contributors are research (MPhil and PhD) students at the University of London Institute of Education.

Margaret Meek, who edited the papers is Reader in the Joint Department of English and Media Studies at the University of London Institute of Education.

Introduction: Ways of Looking
Margaret Meek

The papers in this collection are derived from the explorations of teacher researchers who have set out on the long road of scholarship in the uphill country of children's language development. The writers are not addressing a central theme, but instead they are offering something of their work to their colleagues in the profession for consideration and judgement. The loose linking of the papers allows each one to be considered separately, but their being presented together also shows that researchers, approaching a topic from different starting points, come to find that their concerns overlap in significant ways. They draw on some of the same tap roots of earlier research, while bringing to these the particular nature of their own practical experience and evidence.

Bloomfield called learning the mother tongue 'doubtless the greatest intellectual feat any one of us is called upon to perform.' Certainly the process has attracted an ever-increasing number of enquiries and, especially in the last twenty years, it has engaged the efforts of philosophers, ethnographers, sociologists, linguists and psychologists whose findings are mediated in countless different ways, not all of them helpful, to teachers who spend their working days with children.

The children are also discovering the ways of language. In their interactions with other people and the world around them they make it serve their purposes and learn how it works, especially in planning and recasting experience. Until recently the kinds of evidence for children's language development that teachers have been encouraged to look at have been constrained by the concerns of academic experts. But lately there are signs that teachers are confident and knowledgeable enough to present new kinds of evidence and to enter the debates about the ways in which language intermeshes with the structures of biological growth, the development of ways and means of knowing and feeling, and the child's view of the world. Teachers are becoming their own experts (cf. Talk Workshop Group, 1982). This is particularly true in naturalistic research into reading (Meek et al., 1983).

It is widely taken for granted, and recent studies confirm, that children who have had experience of books and stories read to them are likely to make a good start in learning to read and in school life generally (Wells, 1981). But so far, the early moves in this pre-literate experience, the actual nature of these competences and how they are derived, have been assumed rather than demonstrated in detail. The first three papers here presented look at this domain of language experience.

Carol Fox draws on an extensive collection of children's oral monologues — what comes out in response to the request of the adult to the child to 'tell me a story' — to show how some children, before they go to school, have a range of skills that are distinctly related to the organization of *text*. Here we have evidence of children's ability to use the literary conventions of story telling in ways that go beyond earlier narrative competences. There are spontaneously spoken poems with textual intricacies, 'a sort of collision of oral and literary culture', stories that make clear the children's awareness of the diverse functions of a narrator in relation to listeners, and their acknowledgement of a range of narrative discourse. From these resources the researcher also shows how particular books influence the sustaining of lengthy oral productions.

In the second paper, Henrietta Dombey looks at three-year-old Anna and her mother in the fairly familiar situation of the bed-time story in order to see what is 'linguistically peculiar' about the kind of experience that lies behind pre-literate story telling and the early moves in the child's learning to play the reading game. This is a study in depth which shows the kind of analytical tools that are needed for the anatomizing of the encounter of the adult reader, apprentice reader, author and text. The dialogue of the mother and child is only one aspect of the situation, so the writer unpicks the situational and interactive features of the whole, as well as the formal linguistic structures of the discourse, the text, the various layers of meanings that are generated, and the lessons that the child learns.

From this fragment we have a kind of histological specimen of the tissue of linguistic and other events that are characteristic of the earliest stages of literacy. We see what the mother makes it possible for the child to learn of the processes that will later become reading skills. Perhaps the most important of these is the beginning of a relationship with 'an unseen and unheard participant', the author of the story.

In both of these papers we see children who are having a great deal of adult support. Marian Whitehead, in a paper that retraces some of the well-known paths through early language development, suggests that narrative, clearly the organizing device in the material of the first two papers, is part of the earliest interaction between children and care-givers. Even in early nursing, mothers impute motives and intentions to babies, and as they talk to their children, they supply both halves of a dialogue, so that a sustained conversation is created as a 'proto-narrative'. The problem for the researcher is then to select from this what counts as narrative moves, as distinct from other kinds of early conversational exchange.

Here the writer notes the 'markers' that indicate the nature of the shared narratings. She examines maternal speech style and cultural 'spells' and relates these to the interactions of early play. The enquiry is not exhaustive as the work is still in progress, but it opens up for investigation some aspects of narrative sharing which develop into the child's taking on the roles of both the teller and the told.

The aspects of pre-literacy set out in these three papers revise current notions of what constitutes 'reading readiness'. In school, poems and stories take on the aspects of lessons and development is monitored publicly, especially when children are taught to read. The easy spontaneity of Fox's Jack and Jill seems to be overlaid by a teacherly concern, albeit a responsible one, to equip children with 'skills' in ways that pay little attention to their earlier experience of 'making' the exploitation of rhythm and verse forms – or their emergent literary competences.

The teaching of poetry offers a classroom conundrum. Children accept it naturally in primary school as they have a great deal of playground experience of versifying. Teachers teach poetry 'lessons'. Yet poetry resists 'curricularization' as it is not lesson material about anything except itself. In their efforts to understand children's engagement with it, teachers have to be aware of all the functions of language in speaking, hearing, reading and writing. Poetry has classroom status as literature and links with a lively oral tradition. What then is to be done about it?

In his enquiry into what constitutes good classroom practice, Colin Walter looks at the ways in which children distil their experience into words that are presented with significant form, that is, as something made. The pre-literate abilities that we saw in the earlier papers of 'drawing formal lines round experience' can be traced through the playground language and lore of children. When they are encouraged to collect poems, when poetry in school is 'not an occasional but a regular happening', children retrace their poetic development in order to possess what they know.

From his year's work in poetry in school, Colin Walter demonstrates how children come to an awareness of the formal properties of the language of poetry. As they write their poems, the children show how they exploit the formal features of verse for their own purposes, including the chance of taking risks in public statements. The teacher has to become a master maker with apprentices. Walter writes that poetry cannot be an occasional holiday from other kinds of language development, but must be part of the mainstream progress. That the reading and writing of poetry is at the heart of the problems of the place of the arts in school at this time gives his argument a special relevance (Swanwick, 1982).

The final essay in the collection reminds us that language development in school has its own monitoring systems. The testing of reading, for instance, is a long-established industry that shows no sign of being made redundant and the results obtained are given political and economic significance. Teachers know how well children read. At best the tests are a kind of pond-dipping on a given day, yet they become a 'documentary record'. Another record, the teacher's, exists as an unofficial one. Barry Stierer's intention is to present a piece of evidence from the documentary record and then go on to explore some of the ways in which the interplay between the documentary record and the unofficial record within the research process actually mirrors the dynamics of each of the two classroom processes being investigated in the research — children reading and teachers evaluating their reading. To this he adds the dimension created by the researcher's notes taken during the reading event — a third interpretative process. (In a similar way, this paper 'mirrors' the mode of research of the others in this collection.)

To analyse this layering of significances Stierer presents a transcript of a classroom reading event then unpicks it by drawing on Halliday's sociolinguistic theories of text and situation, and on psycholinguistic theories of reading. The result is a display of the 'relationship between the processes under investigation in educational research and the process of discovering and sense-making within the research itself'. What emerges clearly is that reading assessment cannot be considered in isolation from the total context — of children reading and teachers reading children reading — in which it occurs. The most significant result of this inquiry is the investigator's understanding of his task, the kind of understanding that is denied to the teachers whose operations with reading tests is usually to issue the booklets and collect them again when the blanks have been filled in by the pupils. Hitherto researchers have treated the results of these tests as 'hard evidence'. This paper challenges the notion that assessment of language development can have a self-evident existence. Stierer refuses to accept the usual degree of disjunction that is kept between intuitive understanding of what is happening (so clearly present in all of the papers) and the normally faceless quality of test data.

In bringing these papers together I am hoping that their readers will gain insights into these things: first, that we still know less than we believe about pre-literate activity. Although our researches focus on children from the mainstream of our literate society they go farther and deeper than the events and responses reported by Heath (1983) and Scollon and Scollon (1981) where they call attention to the intimate ways in which oral language learning patterns are related to literacy habits that 'focus on naming, retelling and giving close attention to features of the environment for emphasis' (Heath, 1983). The element of the poetic that occurs in our papers is not recognized elsewhere with the same kind of emphasis (Wells, 1981). But we are still operating within the mainstream culture. We need comparable studies of other ways for other children of integrating language development and the kind of literacy that we have called literary competences.

Next, we need many more sensitive studies of classroom interaction after the stages of reading initiation to follow the examples collected by Wells (1981) and Beveridge (1983). The recent increase in the accreditation of teachers as researchers is our best hope here. Reading and writing are long-term activities with changing processes that demand reflexive understanding for their growth to maturity. The kinds of assessment that are made as the results of examinations need to be supplemented by the understandings that teachers increasingly bring to their view of their task and the pupils' comprehension of what they are about.

Then, these papers are written at a time when funds for large-scale research into literacy have dried up. Teachers in the Institute are looking for new ways to co-ordinate the efforts of their research students who increasingly have to undertake projects either in addition to their work in school or as part of it. This collection of papers is offered as an example of the kind of collaboration within a department that grew out of an association of interests that the students brought with them, and the unexpected ways in which their concerns overlapped to enlighten their progress and their tutor.

References

BEVERIDGE, M., (1983) *Children Thinking Through Language*. London: Edward Arnold.

HEATH, S.B. (1983), *Ways with Words*. Cambridge University Press.

MEEK, M. et al. (1983), *Achieving Literacy*. London: Routledge and Kegan Paul.

SCOLLON, R. and SCOLLON, S.B.K. (1981), 'Narrative, literacy and face in inter-ethnic communication' in R.O. Freedle (ed.), *Advances in Discourse Processes*, Vol. VII. Norwood, N.J.: Ablex.

SWANWICK, K. (1983), *The Arts in Education: Dreaming or wide awake?* Special Professorial Lecture, University of London Institute of Education.

TALK WORKSHOP GROUP (1982), *Becoming Our Own Experts*. London.

WELLS, G. (1981), *Learning Through Interaction: The study of language development*. Cambridge University Press.

Talking Like a Book: Young Children's Oral Monologues
Carol Fox

This is a brief account of a study of the tape-recorded oral monologues told by a small group of young children. Extracts from the monologues of two of them, Jack and Jill, are used to demonstrate the influence of books on their narrative productions, and the emergence of competences which are not only narrative but literary.

Background of the study
Readers of this paper who are parents will very probably be the sort of people who have read stories to their children from the very earliest age. It is likely that they belong to that group described by Shirley Brice Heath, in her recent cross-cultural studies of the uses of literacy in contrasting groups of pre-school children, as 'maintown'. Maintown parents are described as school-oriented, and conscientiously acculturate their children from early infancy to enmesh the real experience of life and the virtual experience of books in an habitual and interdependent bond (Heath, 1982). Whatever diverse theories of reading are held by educators, they generally agree that reading stories to young children is a good thing, that it is a foundation stone of literacy, and of later success at school (see Wells, 1982). Beyond generalities of this kind, however, we know little about the benefits gained from listening to stories read aloud.

White (1956) and Butler (1979) have given very intimate and detailed accounts of individual children's interaction with books in the early years, showing how important books can be for the life and learning of some children. These studies do not set out to discover and classify what the children have learned from their exposure to books, however; they are essentially observations which lack an instrument whereby the children's competencies could be revealed. Applebee (1978) shows the development of a 'concept of story' across the age range, but his data on pre-school children is limited to the one or two oral stories taken from each child in the Pitcher and Prelinger (1963) collection, and necessarily precludes the detailed study of individuals. He demonstrates that some story conventions are learned by young children before they go to school, conventions such as the use of the narrative past tense and openings and closings of stories, but these conventions belong to oral as well as literate narrative (see also Pradl, 1979). If we use the instrument of these studies, that is, oral story monologues, and apply it to individual children whose book experience is 'maintown', like the children in White and Butler's studies, what speculations can be made about the possible outcome?

Hearing bedtime stories is likely to help children to construe reading as a pleasurable activity which in time they will want to undertake by themselves; and most of these 'maintown' children will be familiar with the look of print, the direction of it, the progression of pages, and so on – all very helpful in the infant school. Yet the creation of a *reader* must be more than motivation and familiarity with the conventions of printed pages; the text between the covers must play its part too. It is surely possible, and even probable, that some (or many) maintown children will have learned from the *thousands* of story readings in their pre-school experience many more narrative conventions than research has so far shown; and that some of these, if they can be sorted out, will be not only narrative but *literary*. In other words it is possible that some of these children will have the beginnings of literary competences as part of their narrative competence well before they become independent readers and writers. An understanding of such competences which precede literacy would give new perspectives on reading readiness, and an alternative to the sort of skills usually isolated as contributing to that condition. It is possible that some children start school ready to read not merely letters and words for books, but books and texts for life.

Data

In 1981 I set out to investigate narrative competence in the story monologues of a small group of maintown children aged 3½ – 6. None of them were independent readers, but they were 'performers' of oral narratives, that is, willing to tell stories over a period of months with a parent and a tape-recorder for audience. Parents dated the stories, helped with transcription, and provided much-needed contextual information. No restrictions were placed on the type of story told, and re-tellings of known stories were just as welcome as invented narratives. I have studied these oral monologues to discover what rules for the production of narrative are in the children's competence, and, more specifically, what contribution written stories have made towards an emergent literary competence.

Jack's monologues

Jack recorded eighty-six monologues between 5:0 and 6:1. Most of them are invented stories but scattered throughout are stories retold from books, what

Jack calls 'poems', which he makes up, and imitations of news readings and weather forecasts. It is fortunate that Jack spontaneously varies the 'register' in this way, because he reveals clearly contrasting rule systems which he operates for different kinds of language production. Though this study largely focuses on narrative competence it is worth taking a brief look at one of Jack's non-narrative forms, his 'poems', because they demonstrate that he has learned rules in a clear and concise way which will serve as an introduction to the focus of the whole project.

Rules for poems
Here is an extract from an oral monologue tape-recorded by Jack when he was 6:1. The monologue is very long. Jack begins by retelling a long story his mother has read to him, *Fereyal and Debbo-Engal the Witch*. After an earnest effort to reconstruct the story in the manner of the original text Jack ends his story like this: 'The python perished and that's the 'erished – the end.' This starts him off on a series of word-play nonsense poems from which the following is taken:
(A = Adult)
1. Mummy mummy did a dummy (*laughs*)
2. when she had done that ugly dummy
3. mummy did a canny pummy
4. when he– she had done that canny pummy
5. mummy went to the shops
6. and then when she was at the shops she got herself for the– for the– tonight– for the tonight's meal
7. oh no – it was a poem
8. mummy mummy coming out
9. mummy mummy mummy
10. no I'll do a seashore one
A: maybe not a silly one?
11. a seashore one and it will be silly
12. wave wave go away
13. go back to your girlfriend
14. wavey wavey stop at the seashore
15. say hello to the waving lighthouse
16. waves waves wave good-bye
17. waves waves pull mummy's skirt up
18. waves waves they are crazy
19. waves waves never go near them. (*rhythmically spoken*)

The self-correction in line 7 encapsulates the central focus of my study. What does Jack need to know in order to say with such certainty 'oh no it was a poem'?

He needs to have formulated some rules for the production of poems which are different from his rules for telling stories or talking to his mother. When he hears himself slipping into narrative (line 6), losing his rhyme and rhythm, and talking 'sense', he knows he is no longer making a nonsense poem but a story. He quickly resumes his rhythm by the use of repetition and brings the poem to an end.

Jack has already announced that these are nonsense poems a few lines before the start of this extract. However, he now brings in a different sort of poem, a 'seashore one'. 'Seashore' poems were the first poems Jack produced at 5:5. Here is a quotation from one of them:

1. the sharks catch the fish
2. and the white things in the sea
3. get harder and spikey
4. and the little fish have no hiding places from the sharks
5. 'cos the sharks can easily get through under the rocks
6. because with their terrible claws
7. a– and– and their terrible tusks
8. they can push the stone away . . .

It is clear that the rules for 'seashore' poems are different from the rules for nonsense poems. Jack's rules for the shark poem, and his others of that time, were:

1. present tense;
2. minimal or absent narrative;
3. emphasis on description;
4. use of loose rhythm;
5. use of a soft, solemn, dirge-like tone of voice.

By the time Jack tries nonsense poems, seven months later, his rules have hardened to accommodate a stricter form:

1. use of metre;
2. use of rhyme;
3. use of a syntactic schema (repetition of 'when' clauses);
4. use of repetition;
5. use of invented nonsense words;
6. narrative need not make sense.

In line 6 of the 'mummy' poem Jack breaks all his rules, hence the self-correction. Although Jack says his 'seashore' poem is going to be silly there is no laughter as he delivers it, as there is in the nonsense poems, probably because an overall rule for seashore poems is that they are not funny. However, they have now developed from his previous productions, and incorporate some of the rules which apply to nonsense poems:

1. use of metre;
2. use of present tense;
3. emphasis on description;
4. unity of themes in 'pairs' ('waving lighthouse'/'wave goodbye'; 'girlfriend'/ 'pull mummy's skirt up'; 'go away'/'never go near them'; 'hello'/'goodbye');
5. word-play (double meanings);
6. repetition;
7. syntactic schema (use of imperative mood).

The reader will have recognized some borrowing from Maurice Sendak in Jack's earlier (5:5) shark poem. *Where the Wild Things Are* was a book Jack knew very well. Although he has forgotten that sharks do not have tusks and claws, there is a semantic link with the sea and with the idea of wildness. In the later 'seashore' poem 'wave wave go away' recalls 'rain rain go away' and comes from the oral culture of children. Thus Jack's poems represent a sort of collision of oral and literary culture, a collision which is also found in fairy tales and nursery rhymes. Jack is able to take very familiar forms from book sources (like the Sendak here) and from oral sources (rhymes, jingles, weather forecasts) and transform them to the purpose of making a new form. Later in this same long monologue which started with a long re-telling of a folk-tale from a book, then moved into nonsense and 'seashore' poems, Jack produces the following weather forecast:

1. it'll be sunny at— on the mouth of Newcastle
2. it'll be *very* rainy on the nose of Newcastle (*laughter*)
3. and it'll be *very* nice and silly on the head of Newcastle
4. and it'll be very (*pause*) wet on the tinkle of Newcastle (*laughter*)
5. and it will be *lovely* and *warm* in the *South* of the *ear* (*laughter*)
6. and it will be very nice and smudgey and soft and warm (*laughter*) in the— in the West bum (*laughter*).

Here Jack is combining his rules for both nonsense and 'seashore' poems with his rules for weather forecasts, producing a new form whose structure is poetically organized and whose intention is to ridicule or satirize. Note now that the language needed to describe Jack's monologue is becoming rather literary, because the competences emerging here are not only narrative or poetic in function (both present in cultures which are non-literate) but serve the purposes of reading and writing texts as well — in other words literary competences are developing. 'Text' is a keyword here. Whether they belong to the oral culture or to the literary culture the forms which have influenced the children's monologues in this study all have *texts* which are fixed, unalterable, and repeatable.

Analysis of narratives

Studies of young children's oral narratives have tended to concentrate upon aspects of structure and content (see Pitcher and Prelinger (1963), Ames (1966), Sutton-Smith and Botvin (1977). Because these studies have been developmental the focus has not been on individual children and the kind of data which require the perspectives of literature for their analysis have not emerged. What is needed here is the sort of critical perspective which is not concerned so much with the meaning of individual texts (as traditional English literary criticism has been) as with underlying rules and systems of texts. For example, narrative/literary competences would include rules about the relationship of the narrator to the listener/reader. It is possible to find out if the children in this study have learned to operate the same narrator functions as adult writers use if systems developed for reading adult literary texts are applied to their stories. The narrator functions of Genette (1972) and the connotative codes of Barthes (1970) are both applicable and useful in this respect. (This is not to imply that the children here are producing fiction in any way comparable to that of Proust or Balzac!)

Jill as narrator

Jill is another five-year old 'performer' of oral stories. In her narrations Jill plays the role of the broadcaster-storyteller; in addition to making a kind of text which includes a narrator, she makes a broadcast which includes a story-teller (who may or may not be the author/narrator of the text she makes). She uses sound effects and songs as a broadcaster would, aware that she is narrating through an aural medium. This means that Jill as narrator is using a range of 'voices': the broadcaster's voice, the author/storyteller's voice, the voices of characters inside the story, and sometimes the voice of a second broadcaster (in the 'studio' as it were) whose job it is to sing the songs which are part of Jill's narratives. This sense of broadcasting heightens Jill's awareness of a range of narrator functions which are woven into her stories, both internally and externally. Here is a typical story opening:

1.	Hello I'm Jill again	Narrator as broadcaster
2.	(*pause*) I'm going to tell you a st-another story about a boy this time	Narrator as communicator to audience
3.	a boy called Cletcher	Narrator as director of narrative (subject-matter)
4.	a very funny name	Narrator as evaluator
5.	I made it up (*pause*)	Narrator as communicator to audience and director of narrative
6.	Cletcher was a good boy	Narrator as story-teller

> 7. his mother and father said he   Narrator as director of dialogue using
>   could go to the fair one day   narratized speech.

Jill's story consists of all the different things Cletcher and his sister do at the fair and Jill as broadcaster/author/narrator continues to step outside her story to address her audience:

> 21. and the swing made a noise like this (creaking noises)
> 22. it was an– it needed oil
> 23. I'm sorry I said 'it needed oil'
> 24. we're gonna have a bit of a laugh now (loud laughing noises)
> 25. that's what they made
> 26. when I said 'you can have a bit of a laugh now' the two children laughed
> 27. you can laugh too when you have the tape on again.

The voice of presenter of children's stories on radio can be heard here, but also the voice of the author/narrator who addresses the audience directly during the text. (Compare Jill to Sterne, *Tristram Shandy,* Chapter 4: 'To such, however, as do not choose to go so far back into these things, I can give no better advice, than that they skip over the remaining part of this chapter; for I declare beforehand, 'tis wrote only for the curious and inquisitive.')

Though we see Jill in this story using a range of narrator functions which are found in the texts of adult writers, the examples given so far appear to be related to the aural medium of radio where she has heard texts delivered in this way. However, here is her story ending:

> 41. and soon they were back home
>   tucked in their safe little beds
> 42. they couldn't do anything
>   not ring the bell
>   not play the bagpipes
>   not do the tambourine
>   not see the clown clown clown
>   not go on the swings
>   not go on the fire-engine
>   not pick apples
>   not see the pigs
>   not see the horses
>   not swing swing
>   not see-saw see-saw
>   not watch telly like they did at home
>   not drink out of tonic water bottles
> 43. all they could do was snore.

Jill's mother comments that this passage is influenced by the ending of a storybook they had read together, *What Tina Can Do* (Thea Bank Jensen). As in the original Jill makes the ending into a narrative event by negating all the actions that Cletcher did at the fair – and effectively giving us a second run-through of the story. This complex operation involves powers of recall and summary and the linguistic competence to maintain the syntax in the same negative form throughout, giving a rhythmic, poetic effect. A literary device (Barthes would call it 'antithesis') has been transformed from a book to end Jill's story, and by its means an action (going to bed) is powerfully reinforced in terms of everything it *cannot* accomplish. Thus, like Jack with his poems, Jill's story owes its techniques to the collision of oral and literary sources, both of which are normally permanent as *text* (radio broadcasts are scripted and repeat the same techniques, as in 'Listen with Mother').

Levels at which books influence Jack's and Jill's narratives.
In eighty-six monologues by Jack and nineteen by Jill books exert an extraordinarily strong influence. The children's mothers were able to sort out identifiable sources of content in their stories under four headings:
  1. books;
  2. media;
  3. autobiography;
  4. immediate surroundings during story-telling.
For Jack and Jill books are clearly in the lead:

	Autobiography	*Media*	*Immediate Surroundings*	*Books*
Jack	35	14	0	51
Jill	6	2	5	16

The figures here represent the number of times it has been possible for the mothers to identify any element in a story's content as coming from one of the four sources; the figures for books are necessarily conservative since the children probably heard stories and poems the mothers did not know about. However, it has been possible to identify twelve books for Jill and more than forty for Jack.

The books which have influenced the children's narratives appear in the stories at different levels:
  1. At a minimal or superficial level: the name of a character from a book, a small part of a plot, the quotation of a phrase or sentence.
  2. At the level of linguistic style: quotations or near-quotations sometimes make the source of the language style identifiable but normally stylistic influence operates in a more subtle and diffuse way; the language sounds unlike ordinary five-year old speech and more like that of books.

3. At the level of larger techniques and forms which are found in books the children have heard, and transformed by them to their own story-telling purposes.

The influence of books in Jack's narratives
Space does not permit a full analysis of the monologues, but the three levels described above can all be illustrated from a long story of Jack's, a fairy tale about rabbits, bears, and wolves.

Level 1
At one point in the story a bear character asks a rabbit family:
> 'Well can I stay for the night 'cos I'm a kind bear? It— it's snowy out there, so can you please rub my fur a bit?'

This is easily identifiable as a transformation from a Grimm's fairy tale *Snow White and Rose Red*, which Jack had heard a few times. Here is the original:—
> 'Snow White! Rose Red!' called she. 'Come out! The bear is quite friendly!' So the two little girls came out and stood looking rather doubtfully at the huge black creature. 'Children' said the bear in his deep growling voice, 'Could you please knock some of the snow out of my fur?'

Later in this story Jack draws on the same source again when the bear explains to the rabbit children how he has hidden his jewels under the ground. So here we see the influence of a book at the most superficial level, in which details of the original plot are borrowed.

Level 2
At the second level the language and style of the texts of many fairy tales Jack has heard read aloud is clearly present in his narration:
> Now as you know there was some bears who lived -um- at the very edge of the forest and they would hunt for rabbits . . . but as you know — who lived in the forest? Well, shall I tell you? Well it was a big wicked grey wolf (*pause*) and so— so— so how to get it away from this forest? 'Cos if he saw them he would surely swallow them up . . .

Stylistic conventions borrowed from books here include a range of narrator functions: narrator as story-teller and as direct communicator to the reader/listener; the use of 'would' to establish a past tense which is further back than the events of the story ('they would hunt for rabbits'); the use of conventional elaborations ('the very edge of the forest', 'a big wicked great wolf'); and the use of rather archaic-sounding syntax and vocabulary at the end of the passage, which is close to the language of writing ("Cos if he saw them he would surely swallow them up'). The story also employs a range of ways of presenting dialogue, both the dramatic (direct speech without accompanying narrative), and the

Talking Like a Book 21

more literary form where accompanying narrative *follows* the direct speech as in this exchange:
'How did your mother make that little baby?'
'Oh she borned it to me,' said the baby.
There are also examples of indirect speech (rare in all the oral stories in the data) and narratized speech (the more summarized form of indirect speech).

Level 3
The use of the two rhetorical questions addressed to the reader in this last passage leads on to the third level of literary influence in the stories. Jack is keeping his listener guessing by using these questions. He shows that part of his narrative competence is his knowledge that the narrator possesses all the secrets of the narrative and can manipulate the listener's response by the way he divulges them. This is the narrative code Barthes calls the hermeneutic, that is the narrator's function of keeping the secrets of the text suspended, suggesting the problems and questions which the reader will want the text to answer. Jack's use of the hermeneutic code is very strong in many of his narratives, yet this is a very un-egocentric behaviour for a young child since it requires the story-teller to place himself simultaneously in the positions of narrator and listener. What is his model for its use?

This same story of Jack's has a very imperfect plot structure, yet the whole text is permeated by his use of the hermeneutic code, as though at this stage his most important conceptualization about narrative is that the text should ask itself questions and suspend the answers:

then they were fast asleep but what a dream in the night − in the night they heard big steps coming along they looked out of the window they saw the big bad grey wolf . . .

and well − asy− as you know− do you know what they had? what a dream they heard *big big* bumps coming along and they looked out of the window -um- what did they see? a big fat tall heavy giant . . .

they all had their supper but a strange thing happened −a−in the morning do you know what the− the boy had? the mother borned -er- borned a sister for him . . .

downstairs there was a noise it is a noise that they have heard before −it's−it's of the big wolf carefully stepping in . . .

This last quotation is a borrowing from a text Jack knew very well, *Burglar Bill* (J and A Ahlberg). Here is the original:

Suddenly he wakes up, Downstairs there is a noise. It is a noise that Burglar Bill has heard before; the noise of someone opening a window and climbing carefully in.

Burglar Bill is a story which made a deep impression on Jack and though it is never retold it recurs in his earlier monologues. Jack does not transform the *plot* of the story, but adapts the hermeneutic code; what he has learned from this book is what narrators can do to produce a certain effect upon listeners. He has transformed a *manner of telling*.

Another book, whose theme is closely related to that of *Burglar Bill*, also recurs in his early monologues, usually in the form of retellings: it is *Hansel and Gretel*. Jack tells this story at least eight times throughout his year of tape-recording. He starts by reconstructing *two* original texts he had heard, repeating and echoing the language of the original. But by the time of the fourth recording, some three months after he had last heard the story read aloud, he has made the language largely his own; stylistically it is similar to the original, but more than anything it is the tension of the operation of the hermeneutic code which has remained:

... then the witch said 'What has brought you here my dear children? Come in and rest yourselfs down.' and the— and then— who was very pretending in being very kind – who was— who put Hansel off to bed – she was— she cackled to herself – she was no mo— she was no mother but a wicked – a wickedest witch in the forest this witch was the worst . . .

This passage does not appear in the original text; what Jack has learned from the original is that the narrator holds all the secrets of the story and must divulge them in a way that produces tension in the narrative.

Burglar Bill and *Hansel and Gretel* are both about the separation of young children from their parents, and they appear so frequently in the data from Jack that there can be no doubt about their importance to him. There can be no doubt, either, that these stories, which are so strongly related to his own deep structures of meaning, teach him a great deal about the surface structure of their presentation to him – language, style, narrative techniques – which appears again and again in his own story productions.

Influence of books on later monologues

Later in his story-telling year Jack began to have long stories in chapters read aloud to him. This new development in his reading experience had its influence on his oral stories. Quotations or reconstructions of chunks of text do not appear, since full-length books are not repeatable in the way that short stories were; an adult who comes to the end of a couple of weeks reading twenty or more chapters does not repeat the performance in the way it can be done for short stories. The long story Jack heard at this time was *The Wizard of Oz* by Frank L Baum, and then, almost straightaway, its sequel *The Land of Oz*. Thus over a period of weeks he was immersed in the work of one writer. Jack's own plots became more complex, often consisting of journeys through larger worlds than the 'forest' or 'street' of his earlier narratives; rivers, mountains, caves, clouds, tunnels, *other* worlds, are his settings, and, as in Baum's stories, the tension lies in unravelling the problems and difficulties of getting from one place to another. Jack tells one sequence of stories in chapters and in so doing shows that he knows some of the rules for longer works of fiction. He keeps his characters constant and *in* character, he uses them to relate parts of the story or to tell embedded stories, realizing that once a character has been developed that personage can take on some of the burden of narration. I say 'realizing' advisedly, since what is referred to is a competence; it is doubtful that Jack would have been able to talk about these techniques, but he could, and did, use them. Here are two examples of this development, taken from Chapters One and Two of this story sequence. The two main characters of the story are God and St. Peter and the setting is Heaven — though with its passageways it rather resembles Hades. The problem of Chapter One is the disposal of inappropriate visitors to Heaven, a little puppy who is alive, Dracula, who is dispatched to his grave by God, Frankenstein who keeps himself in God's good books by introducing to Heaven a *kind* dragon, and the kind dragon who is adopted by God and dispatches Dracula when he reappears from death, complete with his teeth from 'a special dentist underground who was magic'! Throughout these four episodes God is a hard-nosed, practical opportunist, and all moral dilemmas are gnawed over by St. Peter. A lot of the narration is accomplished by dialogue.

Extract from Chapter One
    he found a clue, St. Peter did, it was a little puppy
    'Oh no *that* is somebody's from— from— from— who —who's dead, who's just climbed up these mountains and just got here'
    'He's alive'
    'Yes, I don't know what we can do with him, we'll just we'll just throw him back down'
    'Don't throw him back down' said St. Peter, 'We must treat him nicely'

Extract from Chapter Two
    Then the head came back on. Dracula was magic just like any other person.
    St. Peter said to God, 'There's no way to get this evil man'
    'Well the only thing we *can do* is *really* try hard to chop him up in little tiny bits'
    'But he might come alive again'
    'We'll never get him. We'll just have to take care of him. I know what — Dracula?'

'What?'
'You want to be on our side?'
'Yes, I'll be pleased to.'
'Right, then, he's our friend', said God to St. Peter.

Conclusions

The study is not yet complete. However, the illustrative material here is sufficient to demonstrate that children can and do learn complex rules of narrative production before they can read and write, rules which we are sometimes more accustomed to find underlying the texts of mature adult writers. It also illustrates the diversity of ways in which young children can transform their literary experience to their own narrative purposes, so that by the time they come to literacy learning in school they have within their narrative competence the seeds of future literary competences. Jack and Jill are not the sort of children to be considered remarkable by their teachers, and though their reading at age seven is good their experience of reading in school had little in common with their reading at home. The study brings to the forefront of discussions on beginning reading the child's interaction with the *text* s/he reads, and calls into question many of the specially contrived schemes and basal readers which form the 'reading' curriculum in so many infants' schools. The majority of such books come nowhere near using the many narrative conventions children can learn just by listening to good stories read aloud; and they are even further away from the literary competences the children are acquiring. Yet Jack and Jill, in different schools in far apart places, were not usually given 'reading' books which were as complex, well-formed, conventional (in narrative terms), and, above all, as exciting, as the stories they were capable of producing themselves. And what of the others, the non-maintown children? It is surely possible that some of them see very little connection indeed between stories they experience before school (for stories are enjoyed from many other sources than books) and the activity of reading.

References

(a) The Children's Books

AHLBERG, J. and A. (1977). *Burglar Bill.* London: Heinemann.

ARNOTT, K. (1977), 'Fereyal and Debbo-Engal the Witch' in Hope-Simpson, J. (ed.), *Covens and Cauldrons.* London: Beaver Books.

BAUM, F.L. (1900), *The Wizard of Oz.* Chicago, Ill.: Rand McNally.

_____(1904), *The Land of Oz.* Chicago, Ill.: Rand McNally.

JENSEN, T.B. (n.d.), *What Tina Can Do.* London: Methuen.

SENDAK, M. (1967), *Where the Wild Things Are.* London: The Bodley Head.

WILLIAMS-ELLIS, A. (1959), 'Hansel and Gretel' and 'Snow White and Rose Red' in *Grimm's Fairy Tales.* Glasgow: Blackie and Sons.

(b) **Other References**

AMES, L.B. (1966), 'Children's stories' in *Genetic Psychology Monographs,* 73, 337-96.

APPLEBEE, A.N. (1978), *The Child's Concept of Story.* University of Chicago Press.

BARTHES, R. (1970), *S/Z.* London: Cape (Jonathan).

BUTLER, D. (1979), *Cushla and Her Books.* Sevenoaks, Kent: Hodder and Stoughton.

GENETTE, G. (1972), *Narrative Discourse.* Oxford: Basil Blackwell.

HEATH, S.B. (1982), 'What no bed-time story means: narrative skills at home and school.' *Language in Society,* 11, 1.

PITCHER, E.G. and PRELINGER, R.E. (1963), *Children Tell Stories.* New York: International University Press.

PRADL, G.M. (1979), 'Learning how to begin and end a story.' *Language Arts,* 56, 1, January.

SUTTON-SMITH, B. and BOTVIN, G.J. (1977), 'The development of structural complexity in children's fantasy narratives.' *Developmental Psychology,* 3, 4, 377-88.

WELLS, G. (1982), *Story Reading and the Development of Symbolic Skills.* University of Bristol School of Education.

WHITE, D.N. (1956), *Books before Five.* New Zealand Council for Educational Research.

Learning the Language of Books
Henrietta Dombey

Anna and her mother are sitting in Anna's bedroom reading *The Little Red Hen* as part of the nightly bed-time ritual. It is a warm and familiar end to the day's activities, and one that rounds off the day for many children in middle-class families and some also in working-class families. Because the activity is so familiar, there is a danger that we may think of it as mundane and insignificant. Certainly none of the many investigations into child language carried out in recent years has devoted serious analytic attention to this phenomenon.

But the activity seems to have considerable educational significance. Investigations in places as far apart as Bristol and New York City have indicated that an early experience of being read aloud to is positively associated with success in learning to read. Durkin (1966) studied children in New York City who read before first grade and non-reading school entrants otherwise matched to the early readers. She found that the early readers, all of whom were reading at second grade level or above on entry to school, had all been regularly read aloud to by their parents at home before school. This was true for only 74 per cent of the control group of non-reading first graders. Clark's (1976) study of young fluent readers in Scotland shows a similar pattern. Perhaps the most striking finding is that produced recently by Wells in Bristol (Wells 1981a). He has shown that of all the pre-school experiences examined, being read aloud to by a parent is the one most strongly associated with reading achievement at the age of seven. Furthermore, being read aloud to emerges as the most likely candidate for the mechanism that realizes the well-known connection between social class and success in learning to read.

However, these studies do not give any clear indication of precisely how the experience of being read aloud to might facilitate the subsequent process of learning to read. What is now needed is a closer examination of the linguistic transactions taking place when adults read stories to children. Because of the wealth of research on young children's oral language that has been carried out over the last two decades, we now have a very full picture of the kind of oral language transactions that typify the linguistic experience of most children in the pre-school years. If we set against this information a detailed description of the kind of linguistic transaction in which a child is participating when she listens to a story, we can get some idea of what is linguistically peculiar about the experience and what it is about this linguistic experience that might be useful to the child when she starts to learn to read.

What follows, then, is a close examination of part of a transcript of one such story telling at home. I do not claim that this text is typical, as typicality cannot be judged until analysis of a few texts reveals the markers by which this might be measured. The transcript is taken from the first of four stories read to Anna one evening. At three years two months she has over a year's experience of about four stories a day so the activity is familiar, as is this particular story which she has heard several times before. She is also well used to the tape recorder and ignores it. They have reached the point where the Little Red Hen has got the wheat ready for grinding. The utterances are numbered. Their boundaries have been determined by changes of speaker and by intonational units within extended contributions. Exchanges between mother and child are identified by capital letters to the left of the numbers.

Both speakers are interweaving the language of informal conversation with the language of a certain kind of written narrative. Through the contrasts and connections between the two kinds of language Anna is being initiated into a new variety of language which differs in many respects from that of informal conversation.

To reveal all the contrasts and connections between these two varieties we need the right analytical tools. We need tools that will enable us to look not only at the formal features on the surface, but also at what lies under the surface. Systemic grammar which derives in large part from the work of Halliday (1975, 1976, 1977, 1978) is particularly appropriate for three reasons. Firstly, it has informed a number of important empirical studies of child language, which means that observations about this text can be set against findings from studies of oral language development (Halliday, 1975; Wells, 1981b). Secondly, it allows us to dig under the surface of syntax and lexis because it is concerned also with the semantic functions of language and with the situations in which language is constructed and construed. Thirdly, as its name suggests, systemic grammar presents language as a system. This system is made up of interlocking parts operating on a number of connected levels. This means that features of different kinds and on different levels can be related to one another, thus making it possible for one to give a dynamic description of a variety, a description that shows how it works and what is the internal logic that acts with the external forces to make it what it is.

Thus, systemic analysis of this text might reveal some indications of what it

	1. *Mother*:	The Little Red Hen took the wheat to the mill and the miller ground ⎡it into flour
A	2. *Anna*:	⎣whu, whu, why you got a hole in there?
	3. *Mother*:	Well, in a mill they're upstairs and it's like going into an attic and you climb up.
	4.	You know when you go in the attic and you climb up and up the ladder and go through a hole.
	5.	It's like that in a mill.
B	6.	When the wheat had been ground into flour, the little Red Hen took it to the other animals in the farmyard.
	7.	'Who'll help me take this flour to the baker's to be made into bread?' asked the Little Red Hen.
	8.	'Not I' said the . . .
C	9. *Anna*:	I'll tell you where there's thing there
	10. *Mother*:	Where's it gone?
	11. *Anna*:	There's it (* * * * *).
D	12.	'I will' said the fox
	13. *Mother*:	Cat
	14. *Anna*:	Cat, cat.
E	15.	Where are we now?
	16. *Mother*:	We're here.
F	17.	'Not I' said the cat.
	18.	'Not I' said the rat.
	19.	'Not I' said the . . . .
	20. *Anna*:	Cat, pig and baby pig.

⎰ simultaneous speech
⎱

(* * * * *)   indecipherable stretch of speech

. . . . .   rising intonational contour

is about the process of hearing a story read aloud that might contribute to the child's later success in learning to read. We shall begin by looking at the situation in which this reading takes place.

Situation
A story reading like this is rather different from the other activities that dominate the waking hours of most young children. What mother and child are doing is a long way from sorting the washing or building a garage out of lego. Although they are co-operating in turning the pages, we cannot really say that the activity they are engaged in is physical. It seems, instead, to be almost exclusively concerned with language. It is true that they are looking at pictures, but they appear to be doing this in order to construe them verbally. And the language they are producing appears to have no purpose outside itself. It is not merely produced inside the situation. It shapes and makes the situation. Language here is action, not an accompaniment to it.

Situations are characterized also by the relationship between the participants. In this situation the relationship seems less unusual than the action. It has the informal, well-established and emotionally charged quality of most of the situations in which parents and young children talk with each other. Anna is sitting on her mother's knee. Quite typically, her mother is the person with whom she has had the longest and closest relationship of her life so far. But, although her mother calls up a shared experience of Anna going into the attic, the closeness, the emotionality and the long history of the relationship do not dominate this text. Both mother and child are deferring to an unseen third person, Vera Southgate, the author of the Ladybird 'Easy Reading' version of *The Little Red Hen*, who is present only through the words of the printed text, but is nonetheless the dominant participant in this storytelling (Southgate, 1966).

Situations vary also in their mode of linguistic interaction. Whether the channel is spoken or written, dialogue or monologue, shapes and limits the kind of communication that can develop. In this respect, too, the storytelling seems unremarkable, but again only at first glance. Anna and her mother are taking conversational turns as parent and child so often do. But within this dialogue and guided by the text in front of her, the mother engages in some quite extensive monologue, reading large stretches of the printed text without any overt verbal contribution from Anna. Wells' studies of oral language at home show that in conversational interaction between parents and children such extended monologue is unusual and indeed is confined to storytelling (Wells, 1981b).

So the situation in which this storytelling is taking place is peculiar in three ways: it is language engaged in for its own sake, not to further or accompany some other activity, it includes an unseen third participant without whom it would be quite different and who gives rise to the third peculiarity, the intrusion of monologue into the more familiar dialogue.

What are mother and child (and author) up to inside this situation? Is the language they are exchanging so very different from what they use when they get Anna dressed, eat breakfast or tidy the bedroom? The easiest way to begin to answer these questions is to look at the more obvious formal features of the text. But to develop a richer understanding of what is going on we shall later have to move on to look at the semantic features to which these formal features are related and also at the larger structures of discourse which the individual utterances combine to create.

Formal Features
In accordance with the procedures of systemic grammar these will be grouped in terms of their functions. One class of features operates to realize the propositional content of an utterance and so to vary any feature of this sort is to vary the ideas represented. This class is given the label of *transitivity* and is in large part made up of aspects of lexis and syntax, but only those aspects which affect the text's ideational meaning. Other aspects of lexis and syntax serve other functions and so will be examined later.

Anna seems familiar with the words of the text and is puzzled only by the hole in the mill floor. Yet the words are not all entirely commonplace. Such words as 'mill', 'miller', 'grind' and 'wheat' are not part of the ordinary conversational repertoire of twentieth-century British children, most of whom, including Anna, have little experience of the kind of rural life that is dominated by the semi-mechanized activities of the primary agricultural processes. These words all enter the text in the narrative stretches, although 'mill' then makes its way into the surrounding conversation. As we move on to look at the relevant aspects of syntax a sharp contrast between the narrative and the surrounding conversation begins to emerge, and is evident in the contributions of both mother and child.

Taking the mother's contributions first, we can see that in utterances 3 and 4 where she is explaining the hole in the mill floor, she produces loosely structured compound sentences that are typical of informal oral language. These two sentences contain six co-ordinate clauses, all linked with the conjunction 'and'. But the short stretch of narrative that she reads in 1, 6, 7, 8, 17, 18 and 19 has nothing of this looseness. Although an 'and' links the two co-ordinate clauses in 1, this 'and' functions precisely to show the chronologically sequential connection between the two events represented in the two clauses. The other narrative sentences have a tight, complex structure with precisely connected dependent clauses usually preceding the main clause. Utterances 6, 7 and 8 are of this type.

The verb forms that the mother uses show a similar pattern. In most conversations with young children, adults use a limited range of tenses. Indeed, in this text the mother restricts herself to the present tense in all her conversational utterances. But in her narrative utterances the picture is very different. Here, guided by the words printed in the book, she makes use of a complex but logically consistent combination of verb forms. The narrative dialogue between the Little Red Hen and her farmyard colleagues is confined, in this short extract, to the future tense, denoting events which the narrative proper proceeds to present in the past historic or the pluperfect which marks the completion of the grinding process in 6. Anna does not seem confused: she is used to stories in which such verb forms abound.

Her own utterances show a similar contrast. The syntax of her conversation lacks the loosely co-ordinated quality of her mother's, but is characterized instead by a marked immaturity not surprising in a child of only just over three. A significant number of Anna's utterances show deviation from Standard English, the dialect of her home. After stumbling over the initial 'why' in 2 she omits the auxiliary 'have' from the interrogative form. She gets into a syntactic maze in her dependent clauses in 9 and deviates from the usual word order in 11. But when she moves from making her own questions and observations to joining her mother in constructing the narrative, she produces a sentence with no trace of these conversational immaturities. ' "I will" said the fox', at 12, has a complex structure and includes a past tense. And this is not just a trick of memory (which in any case is likely to limit and distort remembered text according to the constraints of the child's own grammatical grasp) for the sentence does not appear in the printed book.

We now turn to other kinds of syntactic and lexical features, those that can be grouped under the heading of *mood*. These features operate to realize not the propositional content of an utterance, but relationships between the participants. So we are concerned with indicators of formality and informality as well as the syntactic forms known more widely as mood markers.

Again there are contrasts within the utterances of both participants. Both speakers seem to move between a close informality in the surrounding conversation and a more distant formality in the narrative, with the narrative dialogue somewhere between the two. In conversation, both use contracted forms in pronoun-copula pairs as shown in 3, 9, 10, 11 and 16. The mother deviates from the printed text in front of her to use a similar contraction in the dialogue at 7. However, contraction is notably absent from Anna's ' "I will" said the fox' in 12. There are no contracted forms at all in the narrative proper.

In their conversation Anna and her mother produce a combination of questions and declarative statements, and they address each other directly. But in the narrative proper there are no questions and no syntactic or lexical signs of direct address between Anna and her mother or between them and the author. However, the narrative dialogue contains a question and some signs of direct address, again placing it between the other two kinds of utterance.

There are also the features of theme to consider, for the terms transitivity and mood do not cover all the formal features of language. When we speak and write, the utterances we produce contain not only features that realize our propositional content and features that realize the relationship between ourselves and our audience. They also contain a range of features which realize the information structure of a text, that is to say, that show which elements in each utterance we are emphasizing as new or particularly significant and which can be taken as already known or as having a less prominent significance. These are known as features of theme. When we look at how these features are distributed in this text we see a pattern similar to the pattern for the distribution of the features of transitivity and mood.

Like most young children Anna makes confident and perhaps slightly exaggerated use of stress and intonation to convey the information structure of her utterances. Intuitively her mother does the same, although she would probably make rather lighter use of these features were she with other adults. In their conversation here, both mother and child use these means alone to mark the distinction between given and new in 2, 3, 4, 5, 10, 15 and 16. For example, in 2 it is through the stress she places on 'hole' that Anna conveys that the focus of her concern is to contrast the presence of a hole in a particular part of the picture with its expected absence rather than with its presence somewhere else, as would be the case if she had stressed 'there'.

In the narrative there are other sources of such information, besides intonation and stress. The syntactic similarity of the narrative utterances and the similarity of the words of which they are composed permits the new elements of each utterance to stand out in relief against the other given elements. 'Who'll help me take this flour to the baker's to be made into bread?' asks the Little Red Hen at 7, in language which bears sufficient syntactic and lexical similarity with an earlier question (not included here) 'Who'll help me take the wheat to the mill to be ground into flour?' for the differences to be thrown into sharp prominence.

The contrast between active and passive is used as a further means of focusing attention. In 6 and 7 the attention is on the flour and the future bread, rather than the miller and the baker who perform the necessary operations of grinding and baking, so passive forms are used. No passives appear in the surrounding conversation.

The ordering of the phrases and clauses within sentences is another device used in the narrative to show where the important parts of the meaning lie, and is particularly evident in the utterances containing dialogue. ' "I will" said the fox', which Anna produces at 12, conforms to the pattern of 8, 17, 18 and 19 in the post-positioning of the main clause and the inversion of its subject-verb order. But in conversation, as Firbas (1972) notes, most of this sort of information is communicated by vocal means, by pauses, stress and intonational contours, as is the case in the conversational utterances here. Of course Anna's mother does not abandon intonation and stress when she moves into narrative. What she does is to supply Anna with two sources of thematic information, introducing the patterns associated with written language by the familiar vocal means. The old is the vehicle for the new, which for Anna has now become sufficiently familiar for her to be able to produce herself an utterance which is thematically structured by means of manipulation of the word order.

So far, in looking at the formal features of this text, we have focused on what can be observed within sentences. But the sentences are of course not independent of each other, even in terms of their formal features. They are linked together by cohesive devices, ties, or connecting threads which act as an irregular warp to the more regular weft of the individual utterances. So we can now see this text as a textile, a fabric of a rather peculiar and complex kind.

The utterances of the narrative proper are firmly woven together to make a closely textured whole. The pieces of narrative dialogue, like *appliqué* motifs, are stitched onto this narrative background, but by the same threads are attached also to the pictures that mother and child are looking at. Around the narrative lies the more unevenly textured conversation. Some of its threads weave together the different contributions, some connect them to the narrative, but very many tether the conversation firmly to the world outside the book, the world of first-hand experience shared by Anna and her mother.

These cohesive devices are of three sorts: lexical cohesion, ellipsis and reference, three of the five features explored by Halliday and Hasan in their seminal work. (1976)

Lexical cohesion is perhaps the most noticeable in this text. Sometimes it takes the form of re-iteration: the noun phrase 'The Little Red Hen' appears in 1, 6 and 7, 'mill' 'wheat' and 'flour' all put in more than one appearance. Collocation also ties the text together. Most of the nouns fall into two groups whose members are often encountered together in other contexts. 'Wheat', 'flour', 'mill', 'miller', 'baker' and 'bread' form one group and 'hen', 'fox', 'cat', 'rat', 'pig', 'baby pig' and 'farmyard' form the other. Nearly all of these lexical ties are operating to create connections within the narrative proper, but one of two operate to connect it to the dialogue and one or two to tie it to the surrounding conversation.

Ellipsis is used only in the narrative dialogue. In their omission of everything except the nominative and the polarity of the sentences they represent, utterances 8, 17, 18 and 19 presuppose the propositional elements in The Little Red Hen's question at 7, to which they are thus bound through ellipsis. Anna shows her productive command of this kind of ellipsis in her contribution to the dialogue at 12, which includes the modal element of the verb but again presupposes the propositional information in 7.

Reference operates throughout the text. Anna's mother makes use of comparative reference at 5 by indicating generalized similarity with the words 'it's like', and also in the narrative proper at 6 by indicating general differences with the words 'the other animals', thus connecting these two utterances to what has gone before.

Demonstration and personal reference are used much more extensively, with over thirty-five instances in the text. Apart from 'that' in 5, all these items in the surrounding conversation of both mother and child operate exophorically, that is to say they are really examples of deixis, pointing outwards to physical elements in Anna's bedroom, in the attic above or in the picture they are looking at, rather than to elements in the text itself.

This is not so in the narrative proper. The word 'the' which in the surrounding conversation serves to indicate specific items in the physical environment, is used in the narrative proper to indicate characters, objects or substances that have been introduced, either directly or by implication, earlier in the narrative. It appears fifteen times used in this way, although Anna produces only one of these uses.

In the narrative dialogue these referential items are used in ways that are simultaneously both deictic and anaphoric. They are deictic in the sense that they refer to elements in the situation, created within the story, which are in every case represented in the pictures. But they are also anaphoric since all these referential items have antecedents in the narrative proper, allowing the text of the written narrative to make sense to an adult, on its own. However, the pictures provide continued deictic support for the child, who herself contributes one of these dual-functioning referential items at 12.

In adult conversation we make use of both deixis and reference, but as Lyons (1975) has pointed out, the two are not developed simultaneously: deixis is the origin from which anaphoric reference develops and this development necessitates a complex psychological adjustment:

> Anaphora involves the transference of what are basically deictic and more specifically, spatial, notions to the temporal dimension of the context of utterance and the reinterpretation of deictic existence in terms of what might be called textual existence. (Lyons, 1975, p. 81)

The narrative dialogue in this text with its dual purpose referential items that point both back into the text and also outward towards the pictures, provides Anna with precisely the kind of supportive experience in which this process of reinterpretation can take place. Perhaps this is one reason why young children seem to have such a strong need for dialogue and pictures in stories.

What an examination of these formal features reveals is something rather more complex than what we could see from looking at the situation alone. It is becoming apparent that mother and daughter are using three kinds of language, each one with its own distinctive pattern. There is the familiar language of informal conversation, the very distinct language of the narrative proper and the language of the narrative dialogue which has some of the features of the other two, and some peculiar to itself. Anna contributes less to the narrative than she does to the conversation, but when she does chip in she does so with a keen awareness of the appropriate formal features.

Semantics

We have seen that Anna is being initiated into using formal features of a variety of language beyond ordinary informal conversation. But of course this text is not just the product of an empty exercise. Anna and her mother are in the business of weaving language to construct meanings. Do the new meanings like the new forms also differ from those of ordinary conversation? Certainly the ideational meanings are not primarily concerned with the immediate physical context shared by mother and daughter. They are not talking about Anna's pyjamas or the toy animals on the chair or the plant on the window-sill. Most of their talk concerns some creatures that neither Anna nor her mother will ever meet at first hand, although it is not clear whether Anna knows this. Admittedly these creatures and the sequence of events that constitutes the story are represented in the pictures they are both looking at as well as in the verbal narrative. But despite the presence of the pictures, all of the utterances of the narrative proper are entirely explicit. They stand on their own, semantically independent of the pictures their speakers are both looking at.

This is in marked contrast with most face-to-face interactions between participants who know each other well. In such interactions a large part of the meaning is frequently unstated. Instead, it is implied and inferred by the participants from their shared physical surroundings, from the focus of gaze, from shared past experiences and from what each knows of the other's assumptions and patterns of thought. These seem to be the principal locations of meaning in the conversational parts of this text, where Anna and her mother are interpreting the picture and talking about the process of reading.

As external observers we can easily infer what Anna means when she asks at 15 'Where are we now?' because we know that she is looking at a book and it makes sense that she is asking which point of the printed text represents the words to be uttered next. In another context the question could mean 'How far away are we from Granny's house?'

And as we look at the bare transcript we can only guess at the ideational content of Anna's question at 2: 'Whu, whu, why you got a hole in there?' In making such a guess we need to know something of the picture Anna was looking at and of how her mother responded. The same is true of the exchange that follows her mother's long monologue. Although Anna's immaturity of syntax provides a complicating factor, it is not the major source of the inexplicitness. Exophoric reference is dominant and not confined to precise references to the immediate situation, nor is it playing only a supporting role in establishing Anna's meaning. If her mother knows what Anna means it is because she knows Anna and has a vast catalogue of memories of things that Anna has seen and talked about that may provide her with the key to what Anna means now.

However, when the narrative is resumed, Anna behaves differently. She joins her mother in making explicit utterances about characters and events even though these are depicted in front of them. This is rather different from Hawkins' (1969) findings with working-class seven-year-olds who were asked to make up a story about a set of pictures in front of both child and investigator. These children created narratives that were relatively inexplicit and depended on the picture to provide essential information. This study has often been criticized (Rosen, 1972; Cooper, 1975; Edwards, 1976) for being based on a situation in which there was no clear need to be explicit, as both investigator and child could see the sequence of pictures that the child's narrative depended on. But Anna and her mother are both looking at a sequence of pictures even more detailed and informative than those used by Hawkins in his study, and yet in their construction of the narrative they are highly explicit.

As they talk together the meanings that Anna and her mother create and construe are not simply ideational. Through their words they renegotiate their relationship with each other and with the author, modifying it or reinforcing it with every utterance. Within the conversational utterances these interpersonal meanings both emphasize the importance that mother and child have for each other and also define the nature of their relationship by implying roles. Anna's question at 2, 'whu, whu, why you got a hole in there?', implies that her mother knows her well, cares about her and can explain to her things that Anna fails to understand. Her mother's explanation implies that she accepts this role, even at the cost of breaking off the narrative. Mother and daughter take on rather different roles when Anna states at 9 'I'll tell you where there's thing there'. Anna is now assuming a role of information-giver and her mother, in following this with a relevant question, sanctions this initiative and takes for herself the minor responding role.

In the narrative utterances there is a narrower range of interpersonal meanings.

Anna's mother seems to be adopting a more formal relationship with Anna. She reserves for herself the role of major information-giver and also partially corrects such information as Anna contributes, in a way in which she does not correct her conversational contributions. Of course Anna's mother is not speaking for herself, but for the unseen author. The formality that is now being created between Anna and her mother through the stricter observation of the status difference between them, is only a reflection of the formality and the status difference between author and reader. The author knows nothing of Anna or her mother as people and makes no pretence of addressing them directly. The emphasis in all the narrative utterances is on the varied ideational meanings. The interpersonal meanings are limited and relatively unimportant.

In this unusual situation and as they move between three different forms of language, Anna and her mother with the aid of the author are creating meanings rather different from those of ordinary conversation. In their ideational content these meanings created in the narrative utterances are explicit even when there is no apparent communicative need for them to be so, and they concern characters and events which bear little superficial resemblance to the world of Anna's firsthand experience. In their interpersonal content there is a contrast between the variation in the conversational utterances and the narrowness of range in the narrative utterances. This narrowness of range throws the semantic emphasis onto the ideational meanings. Anna is becoming used to a variety of language in which what matters is not the relationship between her and her mother, but the propositional content of the utterances they exchange. That these propositions concern relationships between fictitious characters may be a factor that makes it easier for Anna to enter into this new variety.

Discourse Structure
Of course the various utterances produced by Anna and her mother do not stand in isolation, and so to look at them individually will not tell us everything about what the participants are up to. It is not enough to look at their formal features or the kinds of meanings each utterance creates, even when these features act as connecting links. For individual utterances are only part of larger structures, those of discourse.

Conversation analysis is in its infancy. Nevertheless, as Wells, Mongomery and MacLure (1979) have pointed out, linguistic interaction between parents and children exhibits many of such features as have been found to typify adult conversation. It is sequential and contingent and permits the joint construction of meaning. The partners take reciprocal roles as they exchange the commodities of linguistic information or non-linguistic goods and services. The reciprocity of the roles and the constancy of the commodity means that there is a degree of predictability in the course of a conversational exchange. Questions tend to be followed by answers, commands by acceptances or refusals. These sequences are not bound by inviolable rules: abberations abound. But as Sacks (1972) remarks, these are notable absences and they violate the expectations of conversational co-operativeness which Grice (1975) maintains is the guiding principle of all face-to-face linguistic interaction.

The exchanges in this text all appear to conform to the expected pattern and are not remarkable in terms of the roles taken by the participants. Four of the six exchanges are initiated by the child, which is quite consistent with Wells' (1981b) finding that 75 per cent of child/adult exchanges at home are child-initiated. What is unusual is that the commodity is always information. Furthermore, it is not always a matter of communicating information from a participant who knows to one who does not. In D, Anna tells her mother something her mother already knows and indeed Anna gets it wrong. There is no indication that Anna is unaware of her mother's knowledge nor that she is conforming to the frequently found pattern of a display exchange typical of many school classrooms (Sinclair and Coulthard, 1975) and frequently found also in conversations between parents and children at home (MacLure and French, 1981), in which the adult asks a question to elicit known information, the child attempts to supply this and the adult completes the exchange by delivering an evaluation of the child's contribution. It is true that Anna's mother corrects her, but the correction seems less of an evaluation than a gentle nudge of the tiller to keep the boat on course, to allow the narrative to continue in the way in which it should. Both exchanges initiated by the mother (B, F) have a similar quality. She cannot be said to be informing Anna in the usual sense, as Anna already knows this story fairly well. Her mother knows she knows it and invites her to join in. They seem to be confirming their expectations together and, mediated by the mother's reading, the real arbiter of right and wrong is the unseen third participant — the author.

The author determines the content of the informational goods being jointly produced in this way, and also maintains control over stretches far longer than individual exchanges. This results in a predictable pattern not only within such exchanges but also between the two narrative exchanges in this text and beyond them over the narrative as a whole.

This is very different from the patterning of ordinary conversation. Most informal conversations develop by a complex and unpredictable interweaving of exchanges as the participants steer a topic in different directions or change it for a new one, guided more by their own preoccupation than by any sense of a laid-down agenda.

In this text mother and child are midway between the apparent anarchy of informal conversation and the constrained order of a narrative that conforms to a number of definite expectations. There is an agenda to their talk, laid down by the unseen participant and from this agenda only temporary deviations are permitted. This would not be the case if they were talking about tucking in the blankets or what Anna would like for Christmas.

In the pattern and order of this imposed agenda lies a paradoxical opportunity for the novice to make an active contribution, to supply some of the elements that fit into the ordered whole and whose identity can be inferred from a knowledge of the patterns that shape its whole and its parts. This Anna is invited to do. She gets it wrong once, in D, perhaps because the pattern has been temporarily disrupted by the exchange she has just initiated. But she gets it almost right in F and other parts of the transcription show her delighting in getting it absolutely right.

We can see that as well as learning to cope with a particular kind of situation, learning to handle new forms and learning to construct and recognize new kinds of meanings, Anna is also learning to organize these meanings in new ways. Learning is taking place at all these different levels simultaneously and indeed must do so if the language is to retain its functional purpose and unity. For the new situation orients the child towards new kinds of meaning. To realize these new meanings within the limitations of the new situation necessitates new forms, organized in new ways. So none of this learning can be piecemeal although it can be made more accessible by being embedded in the familiar language of conversation.

This is as far as systemic linguistics can take us. But as readers of fiction we know that the agenda behind the exchanges between Anna and her mother is of a particular kind that we are familiar with. It is a narrative agenda and the text we have been looking at contains only fragments of a particular kind of narrative discourse. It is part of a folk tale that has become transmuted into a printed and illustrated story for children and as such operates according to the rules of written narrative which both guide the writer and shape the expectations of the reader. So to gain a fuller understanding of the kind of language activity into which Anna is being initiated we would need to look to such students of narrative discourse as Genette (1980).

Even this would not tell us all we could know about what Anna is learning, for a narrative is only one kind of realization of a story, and stories — which can also be realized through strip cartoons, dramatic enactments and other media — have their own regularities of patterning and logic. Recent studies in story grammar (Mandler and Johnson, 1977; Thorndyke, 1977; de Beaugrande and Colby, 1979) are beginning to indicate the complexity of the interplay between the universalities of the human mind and the shaping forces of particular cultures in determining the patterning of stories. Two things have become clear: the stories conforming most closely to the observed regularities are the ones most easy to understand, remember and reproduce; and young children appear to have to learn about these regularities. It is highly likely that children such as Anna, through becoming familiar with a range of stories, learn these regularities early and are thus better able to understand new stories.

Even if for the purposes of this paper we ignore what Anna has learnt of story and narrative, we can see that her experience of being read aloud to has clear relevance to learning to read. While her syntax is still immature and much of her meaning is incomprehensible to the outsider, she is nonetheless learning to handle a very different set of forms with different lexis, different syntactic patterns and a complex network of connections established through the use of cohesive devices. She will encounter all these new features in her reading books at school.

The meanings are different too. In their ideational content they are more complex, more orderly and more precise than those of the surrounding conversation, although the conversation plays an essential explanatory part in establishing them fully to Anna's satisfaction. Anna is also learning to move away from dependence on implicitly invoking the meanings of the inner and outer worlds she shares with her mother. Instead of relying on the meanings latent in the context they share, she is construing and beginning to create meanings through the use of language alone, even when there is apparently no pressing social need to do so.

It is this that Olson (1977) sees as the centrally important difference between the demands made by oral language and those made by written texts. Children are well used to constructing meaning from imaginative manipulation of their knowledge of the contexts they share with their interlocutors and from skilful use of information from the paralinguistic messages with which face-to-face conversation is enriched. But when they learn to read they have to learn to ignore such sources of information as irrelevant to the matter in hand. They have to learn to construct information from the interplay between the printed text, the pictures and those personal instances of common experience which literacy convention dictates that the author has a right to invoke in the reader. This means paying close attention to the words on the page, and this Anna is learning to do long before she is expected to approach a written text on her own. When the time comes for her to learn to read, she will have at her disposal not only a ready stock of words and syntactic patterns to help her in identifying what is in front of her, but also the knowledge that the meaning is located in what her mind can bring to those words in front of her, and the expectation that they will make sense of a kind that she can recognize. She will, perhaps, be unlikely to look to the teacher's face for elucidation when she is stuck.

But there is more to it than this. She is also learning to handle a relationship with an unseen and unheard participant, the author of the text in front of her. She is learning to derive pleasure from an interaction which lays heavy emphasis on the ideational meanings which are communicated, and much lighter emphasis on the narrower range of interpersonal meanings. Or rather, she is learning that a wealth of other interpersonal meanings can be derived from the interactions between the characters in the text.

There is one more centrally important lesson that Anna is learning. Precisely because her experience of narrative is embedded in a conversation in which she is frequently allowed an initiating role, she is learning the active role in the discourse which she must take if an ideational or an interpersonal meaning is to be constructed which has any significance for her and for the already existing network of meanings that she has in her head. She is learning to interrogate the text, learning that for a story to be created in her mind, the listener (or the reader) cannot rely on a passive receptivity, but must play an active part in the asking of questions, the drawing of inferences and the constructing and testing of hypotheses.

It is her mother, of course, who enables all this to happen. This is not the only way to read to a young child: there are others which would give Anna a poorer experience of written language.

What the mother is doing is acting simultaneously as mediator and model. She mediates between Anna and the author by using the forms Anna is familiar with, such as intonation and stress, as vehicles for familiarizing her with the new syntactic forms. Through reference to shared experiences, she infuses the text with concrete meaning. Through dialogue she helps Anna make sense of monologue. Through encouraging Anna to initiate exchanges she encourages her to take over the development of the narrative and gently corrects her mistakes to ensure that the author's agenda is not lost. Above all, she helps Anna to gain a pleasurable aesthetic satisfaction from constructing the patterned representation of the patterned events that are the story which the narrative realizes. That there is pleasure is undeniable: this text is from the first of four books read that evening, all chosen by Anna, and Anna insists on all four, even though her mother wants to stop at three.

I would not like to claim that because of this experience Anna will have no problems in learning to read. Other kinds of knowledge must also be brought into play. The ability to conceive of words as separable into their constituent phonemes, and to integrate the graphic information with semantic, lexical and syntactic expectations, is also needed. The way in which the teacher represents reading will also be significant. A thorough and caring knowledge of written texts may hamper the child who is expected to respond passively to a sequence of graphic representations which do not add up to a story. In other words, the child who has a rich aural experience of written language may make little progress if she is expected to learn to read by 'sounding out' the early texts of Janet and John.

But if she is encouraged by her teacher to make active use of her extensive knowledge of written language, a child with experience like Anna's should find that she has less to learn about reading than do many of her classmates.

References

BEAUGRANDE, P. de and COLBY, B. (1979), 'Narrative models of action and interaction' *Cognitive Science,* 3, 43-6.

CHATMAN, S. (1976), *Story and Discourse: Narrative structure in fiction and film* Ithaca: Cornell University Press.

CLARK, M. (1976), *Young Fluent Readers: What can they teach us?* London: Heinemann.

COOPER, B. (1975), *Language Differences and Educational Failure* Occasional Paper No. 3. University of Sussex Education Area.

DURKIN, D. (1966), *Children who Read Early: Two longitudinal studies.* New York: Teachers' College Press.

EDWARDS, A.D. (1976), *Language in Culture and Class: The sociology of language and Education.* London: Heinemann.

FIRBAS, J. (1972), 'On the interplay of prosodic and non-prosodic means of achieving functional sentence perspective' in Fried, V. (ed.) *The Prague School of Linguistics and Language Teaching.* London: Oxford University Press.

GENETTE, G. (1980) (trans. Lewin, J.E.) *Narrative Discourse* Oxford: Basil Blackwell.

GRICE, H.P. (1975), 'Logic and conversation' in Cole, P. and Morgan, J.L. (eds.), *Syntax and Semantics* vol. 3, New York: Academic Press, pp. 41-58.

HALLIDAY, M.A.K. (1975), *Learning how to Mean: Explorations in the development of language.* London: Edward Arnold.

────── (1976), *System and Function in Language: Selected papers* Kress, G. (ed.) London: Oxford University Press.

────── (1977), 'Language as code and language as behaviour: a systemic functional interpretation of the nature and ontogenesis of dialogue' in Lamb, S. and Makkai, A. (eds.), *Semiotics of Culture and Language.* Twin Willows N.Y.: The Press.

────── (1978), *Language as Social Semiotic.* London: Edward Arnold.

────── and HASAN, R. (1976), *Cohesion in English* (English Language Series 9). London: Longman.

HAWKINS, P. (1969), 'Social class, the nominal group and reference' *Language and Speech* Vol. 12 pp. 125 to 135.

LYONS, J. (1975), 'Deixis as a source of reference' in Keenan, E. (ed.) *Formal Semantics of Natural Language.* Cambridge: Cambridge University Press.

MacLURE, M. and FRENCH, P. (1981), 'A comparison of talk at home and at school' in Wells, C.G. (1981b).

MANDLER, J. and JOHNSON, N. (1977), 'Remembrance of things parsed: story structure and recall.' *Cognitive Psychology,* 9, 111-151.

OLSON, D. (1977), 'From utterance to text: the bias of language in speech and writing.' *Harvard Educational Review.* 47:3, 257-281.

ROSEN, H. (1972), *Language and Class: A critical look at the theories of Basil Bernstein.* Bristol: Falling Wall Press.

RUMELHART, D.E. (1977), 'Understanding and summarizing brief stories' in La Berge, D. and Samuels, S.J., *Basic Processes in Reading: Perception and comprehension.* Hillsdale, New Jersey: Lawrence Erlbaum Associates.

SACKS, H. (1972), 'On the analyzability of stories by children' in Grumperz, J.L. and Hymes, D. (eds.), *Directions in Sociolinguistics.* New York: Holt Reinhart and Winston.

SINCLAIR, J, McH, and COULTHARD, R.M. (1975), *Towards an Analysis of Discourse: The English used by teachers and pupils.* London: Oxford University Press.

SOUTHGATE, V. (1966), *The Little Red Hen*, A Ladybird 'Easy Reading' Book. Loughborough, England: Wills and Hepworth.

THORNDYKE, P.W. (1977), 'Cognitive structure in comprehension and memory of narrative discourse.' *Cognitive Psychology,* 77-110.

WELLS, C.G. (1981a), 'Pre-school literacy related activities.' Paper presented at conference on *The Cognitive Consequences of Literacy.* Ontario: Ontario Institute for Studies in Education.

_____ (1981b), *Learning through Interaction: The study of language development.* Cambridge University Press.

_____ , MONTGOMERY M. and MacLURE, M. (1979), 'Adult-child discourse: outline of a model of analysis' *Journal of Pragmatics*, 3, 337-380.

Proto-narrative Moves in Early Conversations
Marian Whitehead

In this paper I suggest that our human facility for creating and responding to stories develops out of the very earliest 'conversations' and playful exchanges between infants and their care-givers. These first social interactions are of great interest to researchers: psychologists and linguists locate the roots of early language learning in such exchanges. But these same patterns of interaction can also be seen as the foundations and shapers of narrative. For this reason I have come to identify some of the early conversational exchanges between infants and their care-givers as 'proto-narrative moves' which establish the form of narrative.

The moves start at the moment we are regarded as human and welcomed into the world. There is evidence that the creation of a human social world for the infant begins within minutes of its birth (MacFarlane, 1974 and 1975), when the newborn's grimaces, movements and splutterings are commented on, imitated and interpreted by the mother. The behaviour of the newborn child is not construed as the random responses of an immature organism. Adult care-givers attribute sociability and intentions to the newborn, a necessary first stage in the process of human development.

The next stage follows immediately when the conversational behaviours of the adult seem to be aimed at establishing turn-taking routines with the infant. These moves start with a minimal contribution from the infant, but the adult partner maximizes this help by emphasizing greetings, courteous pauses and endings. These distinctive features lead Catherine Snow (1977) to claim that the speech of mothers to three-month-old babies is remarkably conversational in nature. Some of the commentaries on burps, yawns and smiles are remarkably like little stories or narratives. There is much imputing of motives and emotions and the rudiments of plot begin to surface:

'Where is it? [referring to the baby's wind]
Come on, come on, come on,
You haven't got any.
I don't believe you.' (Snow, 1977)

This mother's commentary reflects her belief that the child has motives and intentions and is capable of contributing to gossip and conversation. The adult seems in no way constrained by a realistic sense of the infant's limited powers of attention and comprehension. Indeed, mothers actually avoid putting questions to the pre-verbal child when it has a mouth full of food and cannot answer — even if it could.

It seems that understanding, intentions and significance are created on behalf of the newborn by caring adults. The crucial context for this creation is the dialogue or conversation, considered by many to be the primary form of language (Weir, 1962; Oakeshott, 1959). Clearly the turn-taking pattern of conversation paves the way for verbal communication by creating slots for the infant's contribution. This form facilitates the development of interactional, regulatory and representational language functions. But turn-taking also establishes the roles of teller and told.

In some early conversations the adult's intention is of a narrative kind, and meanings and messages are imputed to the infant. This is clearly so in the Snow example, above, when the mother is telling a tale about the baby's deceptive intent with respect to wind. In this instance a wholly created story is sustained for the infant listener and probably has a comforting and explanatory power for the teller as well. The adult care-giver is naturally the first to take up the story-teller role but the turn-taking of the adult/infant conversations enables the infant to slot in the rudimentary beginnings of a narrative at a surprisingly early stage.

In one collection of data (Wells, 1981) Mark, aged twenty-three months, shows that he is able to comment on events and experiences in his immediate environment. But, he is also hovering on the edge of narrative commentary. This would appear to be so when his own everyday experiences of eating and enjoying bread are recalled and linked by language to the actuality of observing some birds eating the berries in the garden.

Mark: Birds Mummy
                    Mother: Mm
Mark: Jubs (= birds)
                    Mother: What are they doing?
Mark: Jubs bread
                    Mother: Oh look. They're eating the berries aren't they?
Mark: Yeh
(Wells, 1981, p.102)

Two weeks after the birds comment an extended conversation between Mark and his mother produces the first example of a story in the collection of recorded data. In the course of watching a neighbour gardening Mark and his mother 'develop a fantasized account of a shopping expedition in which he himself [Mark] takes over the role of principal actor' (Wells, 1981, p.106). Collaboratively, infant and care-giver build up a shared narrative. Observations of events outside the window are the jumping off point for a wish-fulfilment shopping spree devoted to buying biscuits and sweets. Other data (McShane, 1980) also contain instances of children in the second year of life beginning to exploit in conversations the power of language to propose future possibilities and pleasures. From the moment of birth our every sound and gesture has been construed as intentional and sociable so it is not surprising that we find it easy to spend the rest of our lives creating stories and sharing them. They may be stories about the artfulness of a three-month-old infant, or the joys of going to the shop to buy chocolate, or the fecklessness of two little pigs, but they are powerful conventions, for they eventually come to function as ways of extending experience and deepening understanding.

The shared narratives of adult and infant call for a constant switching of the roles of teller and told. Such role-switching must greatly increase our feel for stories and our responsiveness to the story-tellers and authors we meet from infancy onwards. Shared interests, mutually supportive routines and commentaries on events in the environment, may be important preliminaries before getting into stories. Indeed, it is possible to speculate that the ability to focus on an event or object of mutual interest and to follow through a routine or sequence of behaviours related to this shared focus is crucially significant. After all, a story, heard or read, is an agreed focus and other concerns and distractions are temporarily suppressed. Listener and story-teller share a private world and the magic lasts so long as both remain involved and interested. When we eventually encounter the teller in a book we must sustain for ourselves the dialogue with our easily avoided or easily put down partner. But we initially learn the moves from an infinitely adaptable and supportive living partner. The forging of a bond with an author, putting the human voice back into the marks on the page, is not utterly remote from the daily preoccupations of young children. Very small children will hold lengthy conversations with blankets and dolls and face flannels. In the darkness of their rooms at night or tucked away in hidey-holes beneath stairs and tables young children weave stories and create new worlds. But the earliest precursors of these playful activities may be the games and proto-gossip of adult and baby.

A close examination of some special features of infant/care-giver interactions indicates the building up of contexts or facilitating situations for narrative. Because these features emerge so early in adult-infant exchanges I would stress that they can only be considered as proto-narrative moves.

It is fairly clear that the first few words of any utterance are crucial in signalling the form and intention of a spoken or written communication. Langer (1953) has drawn attention to the immediacy and effectiveness of those particular linguistic 'triggers' or 'switches' which indicate that we are about to be told a story or a joke. Certain conventions of phrasing gain immediate attention and alert us to the fact that we are invited to participate in a created experience rather than attend to a 'real' state of affairs. The words used are crucial in making the break with actuality; all other physical conditions and stimuli, unless intensely distracting, become irrelevant. It is the invitation of 'Once upon a time . . .' or, 'Did you hear the joke about . . .?' But when and where do we learn to attend to the invitation to share a created experience? Can it be in the playful exchanges between pre-verbal infants and their care-givers? Observations of the exchanges between adults and very young babies indicate that greetings and attention-gaining devices do feature prominently (Stern, 1977).

The communicative repertoires of both adult and infant contain clear invitation markers. The adult uses such special tricks as 'looming', in which a sudden swoop towards the child results in a very close face-to-face position. There is also the use of the child's name, the employment of a range of mock-surprise facial expressions and verbal greetings and questions, 'Do you want to play, then?' The reciprocal nature of these activities is worth stressing because it does not appear to be a one-way traffic from adult to infant. In fact the adult's words are really elicited by the infant because they are uttered as a result of careful scanning or monitoring by the adult of the infant's readiness.

Infants invite exchanges by such moves as the sudden cessation of feeding, prolonged gazing at objects and persons in the immediate environment, smiling and mouthing and vocalizing. So there arises a situation in which the care-giver allows herself to be paced by the child and the child begins to be able to develop confidence in her ability to influence what happens to her. Shared mutual attention is achieved in this way and may well be the precursor of that type of focus or shared agreement which is at the heart of most linguistic exchanges. For many years researchers have claimed that implicit or shared topics about which comments can be made constitute a human conversation (de Laguna, 1963; Macnamara, 1972). Clark (1972) and Bruner (1975) have examined in some detail the turn-taking games and rhymes which adults play with the infants in their care. In focusing on the careful regulation of joint activity which typifies the play and talk between adult and infant Bruner claims to have identified the origins of fundamental linguistic concepts such as agent, action and object.

Clearly these remarkable performances have linguistic significance but they also effect an immediate break with on-going activities and serve to frame or mark out the ensuing experience as special and different. The flow of endless stimuli is over-ridden, its impact lessened, by the fore-grounding of what centrally concerns the participants in the game, the dialogue, the story, or the storybook world. Perhaps these 'triggers' or framing devices mark the access points for a form of experience which is not actual but virtual (Langer, 1953). That is, a wholly created experience which, while using selected features and aspects of the world of shared reality, is marked out as protected from the inexorable demands and logic of that 'real' world. Such aesthetic licence allows us to address the West Wind or a baby's toes and it can certainly accommodate little pigs who eat roast beef.

If, eventually, stories seem to act like spells it really is partly because 'someone fixes you with a glittering eye' (Martin, 1972). The establishment of eye contact is a primary feature of human face-to-face encounters. It is also literally and figuratively a prerequisite for sharing narratives. When the teller holds us with his glittering eye we too listen 'like a three years' child' (Coleridge). But when the tale is done, the bright eye drops its gaze and we turn away. The success of these moves is due in no small measure to those patterns of mutual eye contact and attention-gaining devices established in the first weeks of life. It would appear that the three years' child is already an old hand at the game. In the first weeks of life babies clearly signal the end of a dialogue or period of interaction by breaking gaze and lowering the head or turning away. Should the caregiver, who also uses the same range of termination signals, persist in stimulating the baby despite these signals, distress and crying usually result. Conversely, an alert infant who is ready for interaction will be deeply distressed and even grief-stricken should the care-giver present a blank and unanimated face to her (Schaffer, 1977b). Undoubtedly the first bond with a consistent care-giver develops reciprocity and the culture-specific signs of welcome and rejection, invitation and dismissal, which are conveyed by bodily gestures and physiological states.

There are indications that a special voice pitch, exaggerated intonation patterns and repetitive or highly redundant language usually associated with oral narrative occur in the earliest social and linguistic experiences of infants. Collections of samples of maternal speech with infants in reasonably naturalistic settings have highlighted a baby-talk register (Bruner, 1975 and 1978; Snow and Ferguson, 1977; Messer, 1980). This maternal speech style is characterized by simplicity and redundancy and highly expressive qualities associated with an affectionate and nurturant relationship. It is a simplified speech register in that it features low mean length of utterance (MLU) and is also low in subordinate clauses. But, it is high in repetition and interrogatives and also distinguished by exaggerated intonation patterns, a higher voice pitch and a lexicon of baby-talk words. Snow (1977) now maintains that these features should not be naïvely explained in terms of the mother's supposed view of the infant as lacking attention and comprehension. On the contrary, an emphasis on mother/child interaction as a conversation better explains the phenomenon's distinctive features of face-to-face contact, a context of shared activity, a high frequency of questions and greetings, and such phatic markers as tags and post-completers. Roger Brown

(1977) supports this with a statement which clearly and simply reflects most common-sense views of this language register:

> What I think adults are chiefly trying to do, when they use BT [baby talk] with children, is to communicate, to understand and to be understood, to keep two minds focused on the same topic. (Snow and Ferguson, 1977; introduction, p.12).

The child is not just reliant on a poor overheard sample of speech which is indifferent to his purposes. Care-givers clearly set about teaching their infants to communicate and they facilitate this by linguistically marking salient features in the environment and structuring highly repetitive verbal episodes (Messer, 1980). The primary function of the speech directed to the child is to help him discover his world, and undoubtedly to help him to map language on to the invariances and relationships he discovers there (Shatz and Gelman, 1977). The child will meet these same facilitating features of episodes with clearly marked beginnings and ends, frequent repetitions and greetings and interrogatives, in his first nursery rhyme and story book encounters. And, as the books are mediated by the adult teller, he will hear again the same higher pitched voice, slower speech and exaggerated intonation which first launched him into the human dialogue. How else could one re-tell a narrative which is rich in repetition, repeated climaxes and baby-words and euphemisms?

> Once upon a time there were Three Bears, who lived together in a house of their own, in a wood, One of them was Little, Small, Wee Bear; and one was a Middle-sized Bear, and the other was a Great, Huge Bear. They had each a pot for their porridge, a little pot for the Little, Small, Wee Bear; and a middle-sized pot for the Middle Bear, and a great pot for the Great, Huge Bear. And they had each a chair to sit in; a little chair for the Little, Small, Wee Bear; and a middle-sized chair for the Middle Bear; and a great chair for the Great, Huge Bear. And they had each a bed to sleep in; a little bed for the Little, Small, Wee Bear; and a middle-sized bed for the Middle Bear; and a great bed for the Great, Huge Bear... (Opie and Opie, 1974, p.201).

Equipped with these cultural spells the young child has a powerful tool for handling experiences and emotions. The narrative provides form or shape for confused and disparate feelings and responses. In effect it externalizes them so that they can be contemplated, mulled over and re-enacted. Inner necessity and external reality would appear to be mediated in manageable chunks and in a playful mode. But how does this come about?

Ethological studies suggest that the close and initially exclusive nature of the infant/adult relationship creates a protected setting which facilitates the development of the mastery play characteristic of higher primates (Bruner, 1973 and 1976). Shielded by the adult the infant can both watch and imitate, incorporating observed sequences and actions into play. This possibility of assembling and re-assembling behaviour sequences in a buffered and unpressured way gives rise to improvisation and highly creative combinations. These essential features of play are also basic to language and narrative. Indeed, the young child is soon assembling and re-assembling behaviour and language sequences in his own storying and also meeting this combinatorial language play in the stories he is told. Further, the events and incidents of stories and rhymes are small manageable chunks of reality which can be contemplated, played about with and controlled. This is not so extravagant a claim if it is set alongside further evidence from research into 'mothering' behaviour. In the safe setting of the care-giver/infant situation surprisingly intense and frightening experiences may be approached and participated in by the very young infant. Stern (1977) notes the fact that in games of tickling and grabbing by the care-giver the three-month-old baby runs a narrow path between explosive glee and fright. The mounting suspense of these games is characterised by elements of glee and danger. This same characteristic is clearly present in the phenomenon which Jerome Bruner describes as the incongruous and 'looming' games in which, 'The mother seems able to bring the young, so to speak, to the edge of terror' (Bruner, 1976, p.48). This adult induction of the young into novel situations has had obvious survival value in primate groups and tribal situations, but this ritualistic approach to the new, the frightening and the unexpected remains as an important technique for handling difficult issues. It clearly operates in symbolic forms, such as 'rites of passage' stories and literature, which distance and make contemplatable the strange or unpleasant. These ritualized approaches to the frightening and unfamiliar are already present in some early conversational interactions between infants and care-givers. The kindest of care-givers are often heard to express their intention to 'eat you all up' as they hug and tickle their infants!

The creation of a place in which it is safe to be frightened is a significant feature of the interaction between care-givers and their infants. The concept of an area of experiencing which is protected or buffered from immediate external demands and goals may be related to other psychological theories of culture and personality. Donald Winnicott has sought to locate the origins of all symbolic activities and cultural experience in the 'potential space' created by the interactions between the mother/care-giver and the infant (1974). Winnicott refers to this area of experiencing as a 'third area' because it is intermediate between the inner psychic reality of the infant and the external world of objective reality. This intermediate area of experiencing can be thought of as a protected playground for infant and care-giver in which issues of identity and survival can be negotiated in an unpressured and playful manner. A simple game of 'Peep-bo' with a baby touches lightly on intolerable fears of being lost or abandoned yet immediately reassures with a triumphant 'Boo'. Similar fears and anxieties permeate the art of Maurice Sendak as he toys with the folk myth of changeling babies (Sendak, 1981).

I have claimed that a ready response to the invitation to share a game, a conversation or a story may be established at a very early stage in individual human development. This response is established and maintained by the repertoire of strategies discussed and it is further strengthened by the traditional games and rhymes which the culture provides. Many of the games played with young babies have clear and rhythmic patterns of expectancy and climax, and space for the infant's contribution, as in 'Peek-a-Boo', 'Round and Round the Garden', 'Pat-a-Cake' and 'This Little Pig'. In these experiences of rhythmic patterned language enmeshed with rhythmic bodily actions we might reasonably seek the beginnings of poetry, nursery and nonsense rhymes and the metalinguistic aspects of language which appear so early in infancy and in first language learning. Early infant/adult dialogues rely on the build-up of expectations and the creation of slots for the young participant's contribution. A noticeable feature of the adult vocalization in early conversations is its clear chunking in time and the consequent creation of spaces intended for the pre-verbal infant's 'turn' or reply. But even more remarkable is the claim that these pauses are of the same duration as the average adult-adult dialogue pause, 0.60 seconds (Stern, 1977). Furthermore, in adult/infant dialogues the adult care-giver continues with her share of the dialogic burden as if she had received a reasonable reply or contribution. This remarkable phenomenon of one-person imaginative dialogue soon becomes a regular feature in the young child's own set of language skills as well,

> What the child can do in co-operation today, he can do alone tomorrow. (Vygotsky, 1962, p.104).

The dramatic nature of play rhythms which build to a climax and then must be de-escalated if distress is to be avoided are noted by Stern (1977). They are classified into what might be described as proto-linguistic categories: phrases, runs and episodes of engagement. Indeed, Stern describes the episode of engagement as somewhat analogous to a paragraph in writing – a topic unit. The crucial feature in all this is that the timing pattern which regulates these bursts of human behaviour creates a sufficiently predictable stimulus world from which the infant can build up expectancies. By the end of the first year the infant is usually slotting her own holophrases or approximations to conventional words into the dialogue with the care-giver. The adults who play with the child continue to increase the demand for longer and more accurate contributions to the conversations and the stories. By the age of three the young child is well able to correct a careless or lazy storyteller and to join enthusiastically in the 'huffing and puffing' or the 'trip-trap, trip-trap, over the wooden bridge'.

Once the young child can take on the roles of both teller and told she is able to benefit from various narrative strategies for making sense of experience.

Notable among these strategies is the use of narrative for gaining a hold on the world without recourse to direct action. Narrative, story and book break the stranglehold of always learning by first-hand experience for they give a safe way of trying it out, or, at least, of going over it again and making it bearable. Maurice Sendak (1977) goes back to the feelings of his early childhood and pays homage to the anxiety and the pleasure and the immense problem of being a small child. Dorothy Butler has written an account of the early years of her grand daughter Cushla who was born severely handicapped. Books enabled Cushla to gain a hold on the world, although pain and immobility would well have cut her off from life altogether. For Cushla books were more than enrichment, they were the friends, the colour, the warmth, and the challenges of life itself, and Cushla's books were mediated by loving adults who desperately needed the stories too. Here again, we meet an important function which starts off being shared between adult and child but which the child rapidly takes over for herself. Aided by the technique of storying, she can put it into words, tell it to herself, compose it in terms of scenes (Langer, 1953).

> Now I can read to Looby Lou, 'cause she's tired and sad, and she needs a cuddle and a bottle and a book. (Butler, 1979, p.102).

A remarkable feature of the child's early narratives is their preservation of the two-person dialogue or conversational form. I have already claimed that the shared dialogue is the central feature of early language learning, but dialogue appears to be just as crucial in the development of early narratives. Weir (1962) provides evidence that before the age of three years a child's pre-sleep monologues in a darkened room have a clear dialogic construction. Two-and-a-half-year old Anthony Weir directs his talk to an imagined partner, sometimes a named toy, but he also supplies answers, contradictions and praise in a way strongly reminiscent of the one-person sustained dialogues of care-givers with infants in the first year of infancy. When this point is reached the young child is playing both roles in the dialogue. Dialogue is turning into monologue and the child is sustaining both halves of the partnership for himself. Furthermore, the boundary between self and the world is clearly established with the finding of an inner voice or partner. Piaget (1973) has noted a sensitive record of this in the memoirs of Edmund Gosse (*Father and Son*),

> ... it was in this dual form that the sense of my individuality now suddenly descended upon me and it is equally certain that it was great solace to me to find a sympathiser in my own breast. (Piaget, 1973, p.155).

Granted that these are the recollections of an older child, the remarkable paradox of infancy is clear: individuality emerges from the experience of partnership.

The internalized dialogue carries out the inner speech functions of controlling, planning, recalling and predicting (Vygotsky, 1962) but it is also a form of disembedded language, truly freed from the context of action. There is, consequently, a clear concern with and delight in the substance of language itself, language is played with in that combinatorial and creative way which Bruner (1976) has identified as so crucial in development. There are clear indications, from research and everyday observations, that language is explored and exploited, like any other basic play material, at a very early stage in individual development. Instead of always treating the language system as a vehicle for the communication of meanings and reference, young children also focus on the language material itself. This behaviour gives rise to delightful nonsense words or phrases and minor breaches of propriety (Opie and Opie, 1959; Chukovsky, 1963). It is a linguistic technique which can be used to stand words and worlds on their heads and allows full exploration of the limits of shared reality and cultural norms. So, at this stage in individual development it is possible to locate the early stages of fantasy. Fantasy shares with nonsense and impropriety a tendency to push out or test the boundaries of the conventionally acceptable social, cultural and linguistic norms (Jackson, 1981).

Once language is treated as a play material it facilitates a move into the poetic where language and message become inextricably enmeshed to produce a unique construct. The evidence from the Weir monologues (1962) indicates that the sound of language is the key to this sort of play and exploration. The dominance of play with sound produces rhythms, rhymes and alliteration which then trigger long passages concerned with the passions and problems of a small child's day. In effect, the remarkable sound qualities of the language make it an object of interest in its own right and this highlighting, or foregrounding, of the language forms leads to some delaying of the usual response to external stimuli. Language is savoured, it is mulled over in a way which frees it from the demands of action and the immediately referential. At this point, in Anthony Weir's development two-and-a-half years, narrative has evolved as a symbolic language function. This particular use of language enables us to single out events and features of experience, order them and imbue them with significance. We are able to contemplate and deal with the 'not here' and the 'not now'. In Anthony's case he is able to go over and over the fact that Daddy is with Mummy and will not come to him, that Mummy is unwell and cannot come up to him, and finally he can achieve some sort of resolution and acceptance. Daddy can be present in the act of naming him, he can even be made to dance, and all Anthony's friends and family can be called into the crib by the magic of an incantation:

Little Bobby
Little Nancy
Big Nancy
Big Bob and Nancy and Bobby
And Bob

And two, three Bobbys
Three Bobbys
Four Bobbys

Early language can be described as mapping individual communicative intentions on to the grammar and meanings of the public language, but this is only part of the story. The communicative intentions of the infant are also being mapped on to a grid of narrative-like moves and behaviours.

References

BROWN, R. (1977), 'Introduction' in Snow and Ferguson (1977).

BRUNER, J.S. (1973), 'Organization of early skilled action', *Child Development*, 44.

─────────── (1975), 'The ontogenesis of speech acts', *Journal of Child Language*, 2, 1-19.

─────────── (1976), 'Nature and uses of immaturity', in Bruner, J.S., Jolly, A and Sylva, K. (eds), *Play – Its role in development and evolution* Harmondsworth: Penguin Books.

─────────── (1978), 'Learning how to do things with words', in Bruner, J.S. and Garton, A., *Human Growth and Development* (Wolfson College Lectures, 1976). Oxford: Clarendon Press.

BUTLER, D. (1979), *Cushla and her Books*, Sevenoaks, Kent: Hodder and Stoughton.

CHUKOVSKY, K. (1963), *From Two to Five,* (trans. and ed. Miriam Morton) Los Angeles: University of California Press.

CLARK, E.V. (1972), 'Playing Peek-a-Boo with a four-month-old' *Journal of Psychology*, 82, 287-298.

COLERIDGE, S.T., 'The Rime of the Ancient Mariner'.

GOOSE, E. *Father and Son,* quoted in Piaget (1973).

JACKSON, R. (1981), *Fantasy: The literature of subversion* London: Methuen.

LAGUNA, G.A. De (1963), *Speech: Its function and development* Indiana University Press (Orig. publ. 1927).

LANGER, S.K. (1953), *Feeling and Form. A Theory of Art* London: Routledge and Kegan Paul.

MacFARLANE, A. (1974), 'If a smile is so important . . .' *New Scientist,* 62, 895 (25 April).

─────────── (1975), 'The first hours, and the smile', in Lewin, R. (ed) *Child Alive.* London: Temple Smith.

MACNAMARA, J. (1972) 'Cognitive basis of language learning in infants' *Psychological Review,* 79, January.

McSHANE, J. (1980), *Learning to Talk.* Cambridge: Cambridge University Press.

MARTIN, N. (1972), 'Children and stories: their own and other people's.' *English in Education,* 6, 2.

MESSER, D.J. (1980), 'The episodic structure of maternal speech to young children.' *Journal of Child Language*, 7, February.

OAKESHOTT, M. (1959) *The Voice of Poetry in the Conversation of Mankind*. London Bowes and Bowes.

OPIE, I. and OPIE, P. (1959), *The Lore and Language of Schoolchildren* London: Oxford University Press.

_____(1974), *The Classic Fairy Tales* London: Oxford University Press.

PIAGET, J. (1973), *The Child's Conception of the World*, St. Albans: Paladin (orig. publ. 1929).

SCHAFFER, R.A. (1977a) *Mothering* (in 'The Developing Child' Series, ed. Bruner, J.S., Cole, M. and Lloyd, B.). London: Fontana/Open Books.

_____(ed) (1977b), *Studies in Mother-Infant Interaction.* London: Academic Press.

SHATZ, M. and GELMAN, R. (1977), 'Beyond syntax: the influence of conversational constraints on speech modifications' in Snow and Ferguson (1977).

SENDAK, M. (1977), 'Questions to an artist who is also an author' in Meek, M., Warlow, A. and Barton, G., (eds), *The Cool Web: The pattern of children's reading.* London: The Bodley Head.

_____(1981), *Outside Over There.* London: The Bodley Head.

SNOW, C.E. (1977), 'The development of conversation between mothers and babies.' *Journal of Child Language,* 4, 1-22, February.

_____and FERGUSON, C.A. (eds.) (1977), *Talking to Children: Language input and acquisition.* Cambridge: Cambridge University Press.

STERN, D. (1977), *The First Relationship: Infant and mother* (in 'The Developing Child' Series, eds Bruner, J.S., Cole, M. and Lloyd, B.). London: Fontana/Open Books.

VYGOTSKY, L.S. (1962), *Thought and Language.* Cambridge, Mass: MIT Press (orig. publ. Moscow, 1934).

WEIR, R.H. (1962), *Language in the Crib.* The Hague: Mouton.

WELLS, G. (1981), *Learning through Interaction: The study of language development.* Cambridge: Cambridge University Press.

WINNICOTT, D.W. (1974), *Playing and Reality.* Harmondsworth: Penguin Books (orig. publ. 1971).

Form or Formula? The Practice of Poetry Teaching
Colin Walter

> I too dislike it: there are things that are important beyond all this fiddle
> Reading it, however, with a perfect contempt for it one discovers in it, after all, a place for the genuine.
>
> 'Poetry', Marianne Moore (Moore, 1951).
>
> To make them move, you should start from lightning
> And not forecast the rhythm: rely on chance
> Or so-called chance for its bright emergence
> Once lightning interpenetrates the dance.
>
> Grant them their own traditional steps and postures
> But see they dance it out again and again
> Until only lightning is left to puzzle over –
> The choreography plain and the theme plain.
>
> 'Dance of Words', Robert Graves (Graves, 1965).

There can be few primary school teachers, or teachers of English who are prepared to say that they have no responsibility to teach poetry. Yet the peculiar and intense controversy which has long surrounded the practice of teaching poetry in school continues. There is a widely held opinion that the arts generally (Ross, 1981) and poetry particularly have often not fared well at the hands of schools, and yet there is ample testimony that many children owe a deepened and enduring understanding of poetry to the effects of gifted teaching in schools. For the sake of the teachers responsible for that, and in a desire to emulate them, it is worth enquiring again into what counts as good practice in teaching poetry. What is good about that good practice which entails considerations beyond mere statements by any of us about liking, or not liking, poetry? Our question requires us to focus alike upon poetry and upon childhood. Upon the specifics of claiming that poetry is peculiarly about form and language, and upon a characteristic susceptibility of children to form.

One way in which, as human beings, we seek meaning is by speaking to each other. Form characterizes all our discourse, spoken and written, and it reflects our history and our culture. There are many kinds of discourse and, of these, poetry is but one (Easthope, 1983), albeit an extraordinarily powerful one. It has its defining characteristics, the most notable of which is its dependence upon metre. The production and effects of metricality derive from many sources, among which are the rhythms of the language in which the poem is spoken or written, the ritual and formalities of the life of the culture which produces both language and culture, and the inherited traditions of oral and written poetry. A way of understanding the claim that art, and therefore poetry, is defined by its possessing 'significant form' is by viewing the art of poetry as a product of poetry as discourse. We are then in a position to consider 'how and why significant?' and 'to whom?'

Any discussion of teaching poetry must distinguish and relate the different modes of the child's engagements with a poem. When we consider the pupil as private reader, speaker, and listener, that engagement is with form that has meaning. When we concern ourselves with the child as writer we are not usually looking first at the formal properties of the discourse since it is unlikely that an art object, a totally expressive symbol, will be produced. However, in so far as the child is trying to do what the poet is attempting, he or she is writing towards the appropriate formal use of language. The quality of the work will depend upon the degree to which success in that is achieved. Different approaches to teaching children to write poetry have at root different notions of how children develop their awareness of the significance of form in meaning. For instance Brownjohn's (1980) approach stresses immediately the forms to be learnt, and advocates strategies and games to encourage the reproduction of poetic forms. Ted Hughes' (1967) similar concern with children's apprehension of form in meaning approaches the task of helping children to write from the prior assumption that the origin of their facility with form lies within them; indeed, the very justification for their writing is that it 'enables them to know what they really know'. By writing, the child formulates, re-works, and distils experience by virtue of an ability to be reflexive about how words sound and how they mean.

Here is a poem by Simon, aged ten.

Wetness
Have you been outside?
I have not. I said.
Then why are you wet?
I'm not. I said.
Then what are those drips?
What drips?
Those drips.

I've been playing in the water butt.
So you have been outside!*

What may we say of this writing? It depends for its effect upon rhythm; the nine lines have a unity, achieved by a repetitive and patterned use of question and answer. The first two questions are answered by firm denials, given definition by the repetition of 'I said'; the repetition also serves to establish the interrogative tone of the questioner. When the pattern is neatly broken, the questioner becomes the questioned by 'What drips?', and both participants provide an answer. The final admission seems as much prompted by the repetition of, and responses to, 'drips', and the recalled pleasure of playing in the water butt, as it is by the insistence of the original questioning. Indeed, it is the detachedness of the admission which seems to make necessary the first questioner's final statement, 'So you have been outside!' These, then, are some details of the poem's layered and rhythmic texture. It is both a product and an example of distilled experience, dependent upon language in the making and the presentation, which is neither behaviour in the world nor a piece of isolated introspection (Winnicott, 1971).

How might this poem have come to be like this? Where did this young writer get the form of his poem from? Simon told me that he had the idea for the writing from the kinds of questions his mother asks him. He had, too, been hearing and reading a lot of poems by Robert Frost and Michael Rosen at about the time that he wrote this. We may recognize these influences from the poem's characteristic of spare dialogue, to say nothing of water butts. However, Simon's poem is not about, nor is it all representative of, conversations with his mother, and the style of the poem is only one of its formal features. This presentation of distilled experience is achieved within a context of Simon's knowledge of the significance of form in language. To enquire into that we have to remind ourselves of other instances of the child's ability to concentrate experience, with which his ability to do it in language is contiguous, and to his other abilities to distil experience in language, to which an ability to do it in writing is connected. The proposition is that Simon, from the beginning of his life, along with us all, has been sensitive to the significance of form in language, and able to produce, recognize and respond to examples of metrical and rhythmic forms of language, in understanding his world. Therefore, his poem is connected with previous experience not only of reading and writing poetry, but also with a well practised pre-literate and verbal ability to draw formal lines around his experience. If this is so, the formal characteristics of Simon's poem are but more developed examples of his earlier ability to be reflexive about form and meaning in speech. The origins of this reflexiveness

---

*All the children's poems used in this paper are presented in the state in which they were offered by their writers.

lie at least as far back in the child's history as his earliest production of sound in play; a little later than that his sensitivity to how words sounded was an integral and significant mechanism in his earliest learning of speech itself.

Formal features of pre-literate language:
Our proposition is that what we know about his early learning and behaviour informs our understanding of Simon as a reader and writer of poetry in school at ten years old. In approaching these we may usefully remind ourselves equally of the extreme age and ubiquity of poetry as an art form, the public and oral nature of its origins in the epic, and the still frequently disregarded features of the language system itself, all of which the child is heir to. An emphasis upon human kind as essentially users of, and responders to symbol (Cassirer, 1946), is directly relevant. The roots of speech lie phylogenetically in rhythm, chant and song. Metaphor is part of a mechanism of renewal in the development of speech. The language system into which Simon was born is dependant upon metaphor, which is fashioned and extended by the poet in art. Poetry derives metaphor from language first, rather than the other way round (Langer, 1942).

Ontogenetically the motivations and processes by which the infant acquires speech are the antecedents of the child's interest in attempting to produce poetry, and his ability to respond to poetry in whatever mode of language. The birth of speech in vocalic play, in babbling and lalling, is rhythmic and repetitive, and the creation of words as symbols comes from the non-instrumental production of sound by means of which the child projects feelings into outer objects (Langer, 1942). Early vocalic play in its rhythms and explorations of sounds is turned by care-giving adults into significant songs and rhymes that are later realized in more formal verse. The child thus inherits the prototypes of poetry from two sources, the adults around him and other children.

Simon's earliest induction into his culture was accompanied by song, rhyme and chant (Opie and Opie, 1955). Rhythmic forms are transmitted as the culture is learned. Before they can speak, children hear rhymes and songs presented in play by adults. Babies are tickled to the accompaniment of rhyme in examples such as, 'There was a little mouse . . . '. When they are bathed, soothed and put to sleep, when they put on their clothes and take them off, helpers turn the activity into a ritual with rhyme and rhythm.

In playground lore (Opie and Opie, 1959) we have a world governed by significant form expressed in language, and rooted again in play, a world which the child inherits and to which he contributes. It is a world of satire and nonsense, of riddles, puns, songs and jokes, of skipping and ball rhymes, of nickname in rejection or friendship, of ordeal or companionship within a framework of form; a world where choices are rhymed and counted out, in forms such as:

> Not because you're dirty
> Not because you're clean
> My mother says
> You're a wicked old queen
>
> The one who comes
> To number 6
> Shall surely not be it
> 1 – 2 – 3 – 4 – 5 – 6.
> You're out!
>
> Not...

Such verses are often generations, even centuries, old, and are re-worked and re-expressed by individual children. Children will bring any contemporary experience to that formal interpretation of the world of the playground. This sung example contributed by Simon is a reminder of how pop lyrics and television jingles are allied in playground culture:

> Just one Cornetto
> Give it to me.
> You must be joking
> It's 50p.

Children's love of parody, moreover, reminds us of how they habitually work within inherited verse rhythms and metrical forms.

The consequence of acknowledging that Simon has, throughout his life, been well acquainted with, and sensitive to, the significance of form in language is that teaching poetry entails helping children as readers, hearers, speakers and writers of poems to do what essentially they are already engaged upon, with increased understanding and power. As they come to school, children's relationships with early poetic experiences change and reform. The nursery rhymes can be recalled, but they give way to playground rhymes which normally stay in the playground. When in the classroom children meet poetry as text they are not without experience of poetry. They have to discover, however, the significant relationship between their oral treasury and the forms of the poems they meet on the page. The teacher is the new element in the situation. In school a special context is needed, moreover, where poetry is not an occasional, but a regular happening.

A year's work in poetry:

Simon's poem was written during a recently completed year's work with a group of eleven nine and ten year-olds.* It was undertaken in a search for evidence of, and insights into, children's apprehension and understanding of significant form

---

*From South Park Junior School, Redbridge.

in poetry in the following modes of response: as private readers, as readers aloud, as listeners, and as writers. All the children could read, though their skill varied.

We began by looking for poems in poetry books. Very few of the children owned poetry books, so I made a collection of anthologies for them. They also used the school library and the public library, and thus had always at least three books in their possession at any one time. Every week in the first two terms, we met to read to each other poems that we had found in our own private reading and collecting. Although most of the reading between sessions was done at home, there were undoubtedly many informal contacts between children when they discussed what they had found, and were considering the poems they would read at meetings.

Everyone began to build a personal anthology based upon their private reading and collecting. Very soon, some, and then all, of the children began to write their own work. Quickly, this writing, always done between meetings, became available for reading aloud to the group and for consideration by it. This pattern of private and public reading and writing occupied all of the time set aside in the first two terms, and continued throughout the third term. During terms 1 and 2 no single poem was presented by me to the group and I offered no explicit advice upon reading or writing. No abstract discussion of poetry prompted by me took place. All talk originated in, and was directed at, considering poems and the responses of individual children. There was a danger that any choices made by me, a stranger asking questions, might be construed as significant in ways they were not. Similarly I might easily have constrained the children's writing given the purposes of this part of the enquiry. One of these was to seek evidence of how children were supported in their development as readers, writers, listeners and tellers, by influences other than a teacher.

During these first two terms the children behaved as serious readers and composers of poetry. The activity was continuous in and out of school. Poetry became a natural part of reading and writing. By creating this context I was able to try to lay bare the steps by which children develop in their abilities to draw formal lines around their experience. As we began with Simon's poem, we shall continue to follow him through the year.

Collecting, reading and listening

Simon: 'Two more, just two more!' (Term 2. 18 February 1982)

I want to refer to three features of the year's work which illustrate a continuity between pre-literate and literate response: the chanting accompaniment of children as audience to the reading or telling of a poem by a companion, the rapid development in children's ability to read aloud to companions, and why children of this age are most naturally inclined to enjoy some poems rather than others.

There is a lot of evidence on the tapes that the children's perception of what it is to read poetry privately is radically influenced by how the teacher defines the activity. By inviting the children to find poems that pleased them, I hoped to discover the part that poetic form played in their choosing. The usual classroom situation presents children with poems chosen by someone else and their task is, usually, to agree that the poems are especially valuable or enjoyable. My tapes reveal that the search for poems took on the quality of play, of a playground game. They offered their texts as found objects, and they commented regularly, throughout the year, upon the pleasure of being able to choose freely. Their choosing remained enthusiastic throughout, and although the work has finished, poems still arrive. Their satisfaction came from their remembering other rhymes and games, and the discovery that these can be found, written down in forms that have significance.

We can tell this is the case from a whole cluster of responses on the tapes that are reminiscent of pre-school and playground experience. One example is the spontaneous and rhythmic joining in with the reading or telling of a familiar poem. Although they may not have known the poem well before they heard it, the children often displayed almost instant and complete recall of the whole thing in a group chant. Many choices made for public reading reflected the rhythms of playground material and nursery rhyme. The tapes support a claim that this group of nine and ten-year-olds are still close to the later expressions of nursery rhyme material. Often children speak of their telling and singing these rhymes to younger brothers and sisters at play or bedtime. This kind of interaction seems to modify the earlier claim supported by the Opies (1959) that nursery rhymes are generally transmitted by adults. Transmitted by adults most probably, but often re-inforced by other children, we may say.

When they read poems aloud to others, the children showed distinct expressive qualities. Many revealed an ability to perceive the form of the poem as a totality, along with a definite and swiftly executed adjustment to what a public reading of the poem demands. There is evidence to support a claim that this is not dependent upon adult example but is refined in the playground and transferred to literate engagements with a text. There are many instances of the playground spilling into our meetings. In Meeting 2 Stuart remarked: 'I often think of poems as songs.' There were other occasions when salacious, subversive, or improper material, important in playground contexts hidden from adults, cropped up in group conversation or individual writing. We are inclined not to notice that most classroom encounters are, in important respects, at best just like playground ones. So Simon on the tapes is sometimes the teller or reader and, at other times, a responder to what others present.

We can see another influence of playground culture in children's objections

Form or Formula? 63

to poems. For instance, Simon brought these lines, found in a book which I had lent him, to the group in our second meeting:

> In the park you see trees
> And flowers and grass.

His complaint, 'That's not a poem, it's just a sentence', was really made because, as he saw it, someone was not playing by the rules. At the same meeting, however, his pleasure at reading aloud the whole of Ogden Nash's poem, *Custard the Dragon*, was in strong contrast. His intention to quote and remark upon extracts was irresistible, for the poem contains the clear rhythms which are instantly recognized in playground experience:

> Belinda giggled till she shook the house,
> And Blink said Weeck! which is giggling for a mouse,
> . . .

and

> Meowch! cried Ink, and Ooh! cried Belinda,
> For there was a pirate, climbing in the winda.

Just as children recognize the ritual aspects of playground games so they quickly look for form in verse in texts.

Writing, reading and listening

Sam: If you know what you want to write about you know how to write it.

Simon: Writing does matter because it's interesting. It's important, it's fun, it makes you happy . . . You enjoy it because you have a choice, you can decide what you want to do.

(Term 3. 30 June 1982)

It is worth considering in detail the proposition that the reason children choose so willingly to write poems is that they have already a commitment to significant form in language and a reflexiveness about the meaning and the sound of words. They want to use their own forms and it should be with these that the teacher works.

The freedom from prescription in the playground culture about the suitability of form is of the greatest relevance as we first encourage children to write. Children reciting verses in the playground show us how they exploit the formal aspects of language and what language makes. No one tells them what to do; they teach each other the sayings that are part of a deep oral tradition. The form of the verses makes them memorable. What these verses mean is a matter of negotiation between children, and is often private.

If they are given the same chance to develop appropriate formal properties in their writing, children draw on these memories, rhythms, chants and poems. They also choose how they will design their own poems, what models they will draw on. This will become a more spontaneous form of writing which is not confined to school if the children see that poetry is something language makes according to a pattern that they themselves devise or copy. If children are able to play at home successfully, they will be able to write at home fruitfully. The tapes show many instances of children reflecting with pleasure upon opportunities to write as well as read without prescription outside the classroom.

About reading, Simon says

> You enjoy it more because you have a choice, you can decide what you want to do.

and Corinne,

> I'd mind if there was no poetry because if there wasn't you'd get fed up reading stories all the time, stories that went on and on.

and Daniel,

> I never thought you said, 'you've got to read it' . . . that helps because we thought we were being given a choice.

About writing we have Stuart,

> You can write about anything at home, but at school normally you have to write what the teacher tells you.

Again Kelly speaks of her writing,

> I liked it, it was calm, it was free . . .

and about writing at home,

> I liked all of it. Everything seemed fun. It gives you a bit of an arm ache each night.

Finally, about half way through the year when the activity of writing was well established Simon wrote a poem called *The Fox*. He introduced it by saying,

> I just wanted something to write about. I thought I could write a lot about the fox.

The Fox
The fox moves,
Slowly, stealthily.
A silhouette against the moonlit sky.
Finding its way through the woods,
Its shining coat hidden by the undergrowth.
The prey is sighted!
The fox gradually creeps up behind the prey,
Following its every move.
The fox pounces.
The prey is unaware of the danger.
It is so quick.
The prey does not know what has happened
Until inside its greatest enemy.
Slowly, stealthily,
The fox moves away,

Going its own silent way.
(2 May 1982)

Another feature of the year's work was the interest of children in writing poems with and about each other. Here are two playground games transformed by Simon into poems. The first is about his friends:

In the Woods at Night
Sam and I had a bet
And when we talked my mind was set.
I was going in the woods at night
And I'd lose the bet if I showed any fright.
It was fun at first
Me and a few friends romping around,
Trying to make as much sound
As possible.

Sam's side had chosen to watch us
Just in case they could catch us
Chickening out.

Two other people came with me,
To keep me company
Sam's watcher was Scott
He screamed three times on the trot
We weren't scared.
Scott ran back to his mummy at 1.30 am.
The people who came with me were Peter and Tim.

Sam sent another watcher.
My lot sat on the damp ground
And whistled softly.
We weren't scared.

Then suddenly at 2.55 am.
We jumped up from the ground.
We'd heard a strange sound.
Tim quivered
Pete shook
and I felt like screaming
I got the feeling, 'I hope I'm dreaming!'

But we weren't
So we ran out of the woods.
I didn't care if Sam won the bet.

I suppose we were a bit scared.
(Term 2, 24 February 1982)

The second poem is one which grew from Simon's recognizing formal significance in conversation:

Where do Pineapples Grow?
Where do pineapples grow?
I don't know!
Do they grow on a tree?
Search me!
(Term 2, 11 February 1982)

No doubt this work is similar in style to poems that Simon had read. Yet his description of how it came to be written is valuable for us:

> One of my friends called to me over the road, 'Simon where do pineapples grow?' And I answered, 'I dunno!' And then a few moments later we met again, and we both came back to the other side of the road, and I made it up in ten seconds flat that poem . . . I had the first line already, and when my friend came over I told it (the poem) to him.

My next example raises in quite an explicit way the relation between the child as reader and the child as writer:

From a Snail's Back
Slower than fairies, slower than witches
Slower than people wading through ditches
All of the sights of the hill and the plain,
Slowly pass as we crawl through the rain.
Slower and slower and slower until . . .
If we go any slower we'll stop right still.
(Term 2, 9 April 1982)

Upon reading this the first time I was reminded of Simon's telling me of the playground rhyme, 'Just one Cornetto . . .', which I quoted earlier. We have here an example of a continuity between the child's experience of form in the oral tradition of the playground and his uses of his own forms in literate activity. Just as the child works within received forms in the playground so does he make the forms met in his reading his own. Simon explained that he wrote this poem because he thought it would be fun 'to do the opposite of Robert Louis Stevenson's "From a Railway Carriage" '. Through the year, all the children produced examples of how subtle and gradual was the influence of the poems they read upon their writing. Simon chose the R.L.S. poem as his model and wrote his variation of it. Sandy Brownjohn's approach is to give the children a model to draw attention to its obvious features. Simon chooses the poem that carries *his* intentions; the alternative retains the teacher's intentions.

I want to present two more pieces of evidence. The first is Simon's poem about the amount of talking adults do. He began to read it to a large mixed audience of children and adults just before the headteacher walked in, and continued without faltering to the sentiment,

I don't know who appointed our headmistress
But I hope they know they made a mistake.

In many other contexts such a statement could not have been seen by a young child as without risk. However, Simon perceived this activity as safe, and that is worth exploring at another time. The second piece of evidence serves to remind us that the engagement with this kind of formal writing enables the child to express aspects of personality hitherto hidden. So Sam, talking about the group's writing near the very end of the year, remarks:

> Simon doesn't make too many jokes (normally), and there he is writing all those silly poems . . . which is the exact opposite to Anjuna who is very lighthearted, and writes serious things.

These two instances provide clues about the nature of the child's engagement with poetry. They remind us that, whatever the mode, it is essentially a play activity, an engagement with transitional objects (Winnicott, 1971). In each of the two examples we are concerned with public statements, but they are obviously of a kind which stand in a peculiar relation to consequences and are quite different from other public statements. Children understand that well enough; they understand too that other people will construe the activity their way. It is the formal element of verse which allows the young writer to take risks. Prudence has no priority in the formal public statement which poetry makes. These two examples of behaviour on the tapes illustrate changing perceptions of, and an increased trust in, literate engagements with poems. They indicate that children recognize that the ground rules for reading and writing poetry generate their own criteria of performance and judgement.

An aspect of the children's knowledge which I have not considered in this paper is their previous experience of being taught poetry. Although it is of the greatest importance and significance, it has not been immediately relevant to the features of the children's work which I have especially been considering.

However, in Term 3 the work with the children focused upon the nature of the contribution of the teacher. During this term we met more frequently. Near the beginning of the term the children wrote in workshop sessions with Michael Rosen. Throughout this term, too, I interviewed children in smaller groups in various contexts, enquiring into their perceptions of their continuing work with poetry. We concentrated later in the term on what happened when children were asked to respond to previously unseen texts which I presented. They spent an afternoon out of school with an equal number of student teachers, soon to be teachers of English, music and drama. This meeting took the form of a seminar organized around the children's reading and talking about their reading and writing of poetry. This session was recorded as was every other.

To provide the flavour of this meeting here is part of a description of it written by Corinne:

> We talked about how we read, wrote, described, and thought about poems. It was a bit difficult for me because I just write a poem about anything, and words just come from my brain and I just write them down, jumble them up and turn it into a poem. It seemed a very short day to me and it wasn't long before we went. There was Indian Music playing in another room opposite to us and it put us off a bit, but apart from that it was a fantastic day and I can't wait to see them all again, especially Fiona.

Kelly remarked in the group the next week: 'It was nice to meet the students even though we might never meet them again.'

Another part of the term's activity was with the staff of the school. In seminars after school we explored together our interpretations of the practice of teaching poetry. Readers' groups were established; members of staff generously began to compile personal anthologies and to describe reasons for their choices, and this work continues.

When we read to each other we did just what the children had been doing. The following short extract from the notes of one of the teachers upon her selections may reveal something of what went on. She is writing about just two poems she had offered, 'The Chilterns' and 'Grantchester' by Rupert Brooke, and she has mentioned already how she had always looked for places associated with poems she valued.

> I was reared, by my mother, on Rupert Brooke along with sundry other poets. The poem, 'The Chilterns', was only discovered by me in recent years and that spurred me to find the place. I stayed in Wendover, I made sure it was Autumn, I walked the Roman Road. I found the dead leaves, the white mist, the inn fires. I didn't find Lilley Hoo and, having great faith in the Ordnance Survey, hereby accuse Brooke of trickery. But all the rest is there.
>
> As for 'Grantchester', well, that really is special to me. It was the poem and my mother's influence that got me there originally. Since then, other associations have increased its importance. I could recite the whole poem by heart, but I don't intend to type it all: it's very long. So this is just the final part. In it Brooke asks a number of questions about the area. Two years ago I checked them all out, and can answer yes to all except the church clock one: I even saw the hares.

Implications for good practice

We have to recognize ways in which classrooms are just like playgrounds and ways in which they are not, in this matter of teaching children poetry. Our consideration of the significance of form to children, and of their engagement with significant form in language, implies that teaching poetry obliges us to seek continuity between children's pre-literate and literate experiences of form. That is the teacher's peculiar contribution. Children have a commitment to making and using objects in language. They are well versed at home, and in the playground, in how to recognize, organize and formally arrange, speech in prototypes of expressive symbols.

The next, and related, implication of what I have tried to argue, for good practice, is that we acknowledge and seek to understand better the complexity of the relation between the achievement by the child of form in the literate modes of reading and writing poems. There is an imperative not to underestimate the importance of the gradual and sustained influence of forms read upon forms written. We need to develop long-term intentions towards, and strategies for, achieving the parallel development of children's reading and writing in this area. The ways in which children's reading affects writing are legion, and often operate beneath a conscious level. As I have already implied, poetic forms are not as easily, nor often always as usefully, abstracted by the teacher for use by the child as is sometimes assumed (Brownjohn, 1980). Unless such exercises are broadly contextualized within catholic, freely chosen, and continuous reading and writing activity, the writing achieved may be constrained by formula rather than enlivened by form.

Acknowledging children's reading and writing poems as important because they are essentially play, in the sense described by D.W. Winnicott (1971), implies the need to encourage children to write, as well as read, outside the classroom, as well as inside. Further, it suggests a value in doing so for pleasure, and from choice, in the same contexts wherein they learnt previously to use their own voices and forms within the constraints and possibilities of inherited form.

These long term approaches are the best safeguards against the teaching of poetry becoming curriculumized, a process by which poetry becomes so accepted as valuable to children, by us as teachers, that the natural difficulties and uncertainties about the precise nature of its value are hidden. We have to contextualize the poetry lesson. In ending, I want to refer to one more poem and another conversation. So, first the poem, which is by Corinne:

The Sulk*
I'm in a sulk.

---

*I would like to thank Michael Rosen for permission to use this poem.

An angry sulk.
Can't have an ice-cream.
It's not fair —
Mum says I ain't allowed to have an ice-cream
For a whole week,
Imagine that, no ice-cream
For a whole week.

I'm in a sulk.
An angry sulk.
Can't play out.
It's not fair —
Mum says I ain't allowed to play out
For a whole week
Imagine that, no playing out
For a whole week.

I'm in a sulk.
An angry sulk.
Can't play me organ.
It's not fair —
Mum says I ain't allowed to play my organ
For a whole week.

Can't do nuffin in this 'ouse.

(Term 3. 24 May 1982)

The conversation, similarly, suggests a widening focus, and echoes, too, the main theme of this paper. It is between a small group discussing their pleasure in being able to write at home. It ends, and so shall I, with Sam describing its value for him.

Sam: It's very different . . . the more time you get, the more ideas you get.
Shoab: At home you have more in your head, and you know what to write about.
Sam: Also, at school you're not just writing *that* piece of work . . . 'Oh no! we've got maths this afternoon! I haven't done my tables!' . . . All these things are going through your mind, it takes your concentration off. At home you're free to do it.
Anjuna: It helps you to write in your own way and with your own choices . . . like Mr. Rosen. He developed his own way of writing a poem . . .
Shoab: It does matter, it amuses you.
Sam: . . . You can let your imagination run wild. I think it important that you shouldn't always do what you're told in writing. You ought to be allowed to write what you want. If you are told all your life to do exactly what other people tell you, then you'll find that you won't have anything to show that's really yours.

(Term 3. 24 May 1982)

Form or Formula? 71

Summary

My concern in this paper has been with the nature of good practice in teaching children poetry. That concern necessarily involves approaching the controversial question of how children gain an understanding of literary form. To this end I have suggested the relevance of a view of poetry as discourse which may become art, and that when children write and read poems regularly, understanding develops as a by-product of an intention to seek and find meaning within specific sets of conventions.

A phylogenetic enquiry into poetry runs us straight back to its early forms, the epic for instance. The pre-literate experience of children in play, their production of sound within the mechanism of speech acquisition, and nursery and playground lore, provide us with evidence of the importance of poetry to children. At school the child meets poetry as text, and we thus have to find a special contribution for the teacher to make. In introducing a year's work with children I have attempted to contextualize *the poetry lesson*; in doing so I have argued for a need to establish a continuity between pre-literate and literate engagements with poetry, and to pursue the details of how children's reading helps their writing and vice-versa.

References

BROWNJOHN, S. (1980), *Does it Have to Rhyme?* Sevenoaks, Kent: Hodder and Stoughton.

CASSIRER, E. (1946), *Language and Myth*. New York: Dover.

EASTHOPE, A. (1983), *Poetry as Discourse*. London: Methuen.

GRAVES, R. (1965), *Collected Poems*. London: Cassell.

HUGHES, T. (1967), *Poetry in the Making*. London: Faber and Faber.

LANGER, S. (1942), *Philosophy in a New Key*. Cambridge, Mass: Harvard Univesity Press.

────── (1953), *Feeling and Form*. London: Routledge and Kegan Paul.

MOORE, M. (1951), *Collected Poems*. London: Faber and Faber.

OPIE, I. and OPIE, P. (1955), *The Oxford Nursery Rhyme Book*. London: Oxford University Press.

────── (1959), *The Lore and Language of Schoolchildren*. London: Oxford University Press.

ROSS, M. (ed) (1981), *The Aesthetic Imperative*. Oxford: Pergamon Press.

WINNICOTT, D.W. (1971), *Playing and Reality*. London: Tavistock Publications.

A Researcher Reading Teachers Reading Children Reading
Notes on the task of making sense of reading assessment in the classroom
Barry Stierer

> ... the social scientist of necessity draws upon the same sorts of skills as those whose conduct he seeks to analyse in order to describe it...
> Anthony Giddens, *New Rules of Sociological Method* (1976, p.155).

> ... anyone concerned with the interaction of groups and individuals may find in the act of reading the basic principles that govern the human activities he studies; for reading ever so curiously mingles person and thing and person and person.
> Norman Holland, *Five Readers Reading* (1975, p.xiii).

Can research tell us anything new about the teaching and learning of reading in schools? Perhaps not, but then what we normally mean by 'reading research' is a collection of findings. The *process* by which those findings are achieved, and especially the researcher's own experience of carrying out the investigation, are inevitably relegated to the category of 'methodology', over-shadowed by the more substantive concerns of the project. This paper explores the notion that some of the most important things to be said about children and teachers engaged in 'reading' at school are best expressed in terms of how they were found out.

I have recently had the good fortune to spend two terms carrying out participant/observation research in three first-year junior classes. My brief was to collect as much detailed 'data' as possible related to teachers' everyday practices for evaluating children's reading in the classroom. I worked closely with the three teachers, studying the complex process by which they came to 'know' their pupils as readers: what they looked for; when, where and how they looked; why they looked for certain things at certain times; what kinds of judgements they formed about children as readers; and what actions they took on the basis of these judgements. Ultimately I wanted to see what kind of relationship emerged between teachers' assessment practices and their teaching of reading.

With the field work in schools finished, the collection of 'data' just referred to falls into two categories. The first category is the tangible, documentary record, consisting of: field notes taken during observations of teachers and children working right across the range of school activity; many hours of tape-recorded classroom talk; and the notes and tape-recordings arising from many discussions with the classroom teachers. The second category of the data consists of my own personal 'feel' for the events recorded in the documentary record, which is the result of my having been an active participant within them. This second, unofficial record is what Charles Hull (1981) calls the 'black market record': the 'understandings built up over time and carried in [the researcher's] head' (p. 1). The tangible record — the notes and tapes — are evocative of those classroom events which the researcher observed and took part in, but fall short of 'telling the story': of conveying the meanings which the researcher became party to as the project progressed. The unofficial record, based on the researcher's familiarity with the unique lore of the three classrooms, is the corpus of evidence which transforms the first record into a living story, but which is too personal to be easily verifiable or even communicated to others.

The starting point for this paper, then, is the dilemma facing the researcher attempting to resolve the tension between these two categories of data. With the more reliable, but two-dimensional, documents of the first record on the one hand, and the highly personal and intuitive, but undocumented, second record on the other, what strategy should the researcher adopt to produce the fullest and yet the most valid account and analysis?

I shall present a piece of evidence from the documentary record, and then go on to explore some of the ways in which the interplay between the documentary record and the unofficial record within the research process actually mirrors the dynamics of each of the two classroom processes being investigated in the research — children reading and teachers evaluating their reading.

This piece of evidence is an excerpt from a transcript of a tape-recording made in a first-year junior class. The event this transcript relates to is a fairly routine (for this class) reading session: children are reading quietly from their reading books at their tables and queueing up to the teacher at her desk either for help with difficult words or to be 'checked' on a book they have finished in order to be given their next book. The excerpt begins when the session has been formally in progress for about three minutes: most children have settled to their books, a queue has formed and the teacher is finishing up some administrative business before dealing with Colin[1] who stands at the head of the queue with his finished reading book.[2]

    Ms Harvey: Has Julie gone?
    several pupils
    at once: Yes . . . Yes.
    Ms Harvey: Oh, well, in that case Patrick would you like to take that clock back to Mrs Arthur and say Ms Harvey says 'thank you'?

Patrick:	Yes.
Ms Harvey:	(*after pause*) Right. Now ... You *should* be reading your reading book ...
pupil:	(*barely audible*) I'm not.
Ms Harvey:	(*after pause of six seconds*) If I heard a person say 'I'm not' I want to know the reason why.
Colin:	(*after long pause, begins reading*) Brasilia ...
Ms Harvey:	No, from here please.
Colin:	(*begins again*) The people of Brazil nearly all lived along the sea coast. The new city was built far / / island (*miscues* 'inland') / / inland (*self-corrects*) on a road / / ha / / ha / /
Lucie:	(*interrupting*) My finger hurts.
Ms Harvey:	Oh, *tough*. Would you like me to chop it off?
Colin:	(*trying to continue reading*) ha / / ha
Lucie:	No.
Ms Harvey:	Can't do anything about it, other than chop it off. (*To Colin, as prompt*) ... road? ...
Colin:	ha / / ha / /
Ms Harvey:	Well, pretend that's a 'b' ... what would it say?
Colin:	back.
Ms Harvey:	Right. Now, change it to an 'h'.
Colin:	hack.
Ms Harvey:	hack? ...
Colin:	hacked through the steaming jungle. It is a city of—of concrete and marble and glass. There are no traffic lights, for every cross-roads (*miscues* 'crossroad') is a flyover or an underpass. There are great blocks of – There are great blocks of ...
Ms Harvey:	(*whispering to another pupil*) Oh, thanks very much.
Colin:	well painted (*miscues* 'planned') offices. There is a cathedral. There are churches and schools and shopping centres free from traffic. There are green / / lawns and bright, tropical flowers, – and there are people. Thousands and thousands of men, women and children have flocked to (*inserts* 'see') the country's new capital. They have come from poor, dusty villages and crowded / / seaports. They have found homes and work and friends. They have brought life to Brasilia.
Ms Harvey:	Right. Now, that's fine. Now, have you picked out a story from that?
Colin:	Uh, no.
Ms Harvey:	Pick out a story that you particularly enjoyed and just write a

> brief account of it for me please. All right?
> Colin: Can I do this one, 'cos I . . .
> Ms Harvey: Well, if you, if you want to, but don't copy it will you?
> (*To Thomas, next child in queue*) Yes?

How can the researcher go about achieving an understanding of 'what happened' in this scene? How can he be certain that the meaning he does manage to extract from (or read into!) this short fragment does not merely reflect 'the pattern of the researcher's head' (Willis, 1976, p. 136)? And how can he communicate his analysis to those who did not participate in the event being examined, while still preserving both the authority of the 'documentary record' as well as the immediacy of the 'unofficial record'?

Layers of evidence

These questions become critical when applied specifically to the task of analysing this classroom scene in terms of its significance for the assessment of reading. What counts as reading assessment here, and how can it be interpreted? What reading assessment there *is* going on seems so deeply embedded in the fabric of meaning in the classroom that it is difficult to tease out its particular significance.

We can begin an analysis of this scene by looking at the first part of the 'documentary' record — the transcript of the tape-recording. The story which the transcript tells only breaks the surface of the layers of meaning operating here: 'teacher finishes administrative business; teacher reinforces the instruction which defines the terms of the lesson; teacher listens to pupil's oral reading; pupil is interrupted by another pupil who is dealt with by the teacher; pupil continues reading; teacher intervenes when pupil encounters difficulty; teacher closes interaction with pupil and issues writing assignment.' Of course there is much more we can glean from the transcript by careful scrutiny. We can gain a sense of the rules which govern the various interactions between teacher and pupils; we can see that those rules are formally mediated by the teacher; we can gain a sense of the acceptable level of sarcasm permitted in the classroom; we can observe the teacher's techniques for coping with conflicting demands on her time; and we can formulate hypotheses about what the teacher is 'doing' as she listens to Colin's reading.

The transcript, however, is only the starting point of an analysis of what reading assessment transpires between Ms Harvey and Colin. From the transcript we can consult the other part of the documentary record, the observation notes. The notes 'show' that Ms Harvey and Colin are holding the book together; that Ms Harvey uses Colin's Reading Record as a marker, moving it down line-by-line as Colin reads; that Ms Harvey occasionally points to words in Colin's book with her pen as a silent prompt, which of course is not picked up on the tape; that the queue builds up, as Colin reads, to as may as six or seven children; that a parent volunteer enters the room while Colin is reading, sets herself up in one corner of the classroom, and proceeds to call the first child on the list of children whom she hears read on a weekly basis; that the head teacher has come into the room and is standing at Ms Harvey's desk waiting for an opportunity to speak to her.

But of course the researcher's notes taken during the event are by no means an objective record or account of 'what happened'; neither do they really 'speak for themselves'. They are the outcome of a highly selective and interpretive process, shaped to a large extent by the researcher's prior knowledge of the teacher and the pupils, by his own relationships with them and by his accumulated understanding of what he might expect to have happened in the event recorded in the observation notes. The notes are also shaped by the researcher's own idea of what a researcher's observation notes ought to look like. They are therefore in one sense a crude record of his own experience of the event.

It is, however, only when we begin to consult the 'black market record' – the researcher's own personal understanding of the meanings operating in this scene – that we begin to 'know' what is happening. The 'black market record' suggests that this lesson has a familiar and well-defined structure, and that Ms Harvey's reinforcement, 'You *should* be reading your reading book', is sufficient to signify to the class that this structure has taken effect; that Ms Harvey considers Colin to be a technically fluent but uninspired reader; that Ms Harvey and Colin know that permission to move on to the next reading book is contingent on (i) an oral rendition by Colin of part of the final chapter in the reading book, during which he should not get 'stuck' too often, and (ii) the completion of the short piece of writing she assigns him; and that the likely object of the head teacher's visit is to follow up a complaint Ms Harvey had made to him that morning. These 'black market' aspects of the event are either entirely absent from the transcript or only remotely implied within it, and yet the researcher will be vividly aware of them as he 'reads' the transcript. Furthermore, his analysis of this event, months after it happened, will draw on the knowledge and relationships which he built up in the classroom subsequent to the event, as well as on the working environment in which that later analysis is carried out. To what extent, for example, will his analysis of the scene's significance for reading assessment be shaped by his knowledge in hindsight of Ms Harvey's more recent views about Colin's reading, expressed to the researcher, or indeed by the pressures brought to bear on the researcher to report his findings impersonally? None of these are explicit aspects of the documentary record, but they are almost impossible to exclude from an analysis of the event.

The text and situation of data

One possible exit from this quandary is provided by sociolinguists in their analysis of the relationship between language and the setting in which language is used. Michael Halliday, for example, develops the notions of 'text' and 'situation'. He defines 'text' as 'the instances of linguistic interaction in which people actually engage: whatever is said, or written, in an operational context' (1978, pp. 108-9). Elsewhere (1976, p. 123) he writes that the term 'text'

> covers both speech and writing, and is quite neutral as regards style and content: it may be language in action, conversation, telephone talk, debate, dramatic dialogue, narrative fiction, poetry, prayer, inscriptions, public notices, legal proceedings, communicating with animals, intimate monologue or anything else.

'Situation' on the other hand is seen as 'the environment in which the text comes to life' (1978, p. 109). Although to Halliday it is possible to identify *types* of situations governed by rules of communication derived from wider social and cultural structures, Edwards and Furlong (1978) warn (pp. 55-6).

> ... that context should not be used as an ill-defined and static dumping ground for what the participants are supposed to know about that part of their social world. The relevant context changes rapidly.

Sociolinguists agree, however, that text and situation are part of all language and are inseparable features of all language.

Sociolinguistic theories of text and situation provide an extremely useful model for describing the relationship between the 'documentary record' and the 'unofficial record' in the present research on reading assessment. The more tangible kinds of evidence − the observation notes, the tapes, the transcripts − are all examples of language in operational contexts and therefore qualify as 'texts'. The inexplicit element of the text − the researcher's familiarity with the structure and meaning of the social situation in which the text was produced − is an example of Halliday's notion of 'situation'. Halliday writes:

> If it is true that a hearer, given the right information, can make sensible guesses about what the speaker is going to mean − and this seems a necessary assumption seeing that communication does take place − then this 'right information' is what we mean by the social context. *It consists of those general properties of the situation which collectively function as the determinants of text.* (1978, p. 110) (my italic)

If we replace 'hearer' and 'speaker' with 'language producer' and 'language receiver' − and this is justifiable since 'text' embraces written as well as spoken language − this passage provides a serviceable description of the analytic process in case-study research. Tapes and field notes, for example, however revealing as texts, are unable to convey the 'general properties of the situation which collectively function as the determinants of text'. The type of interaction between Ms Harvey and Colin on the tape transcript may be recognizable as 'teacher hearing pupil read' but only the researcher would be able to describe the special structure and significance of the lesson which Ms Harvey inaugurates with the words, '*Right. Now . . .* You *should* be reading your reading book.' This unofficial data is the 'right information' which renders a text intelligible. Similarly, the researcher's observation notes, of the interaction between Colin and Ms Harvey, are ultimately texts communicated by the researcher to himself for reading at a later date. In order for the 'communication to take place' – in order for the 'hearer' to make 'sensible guesses about what the speaker is going to mean' – 'and in order for the researcher to make sense of his own observation notes, he must make use of the 'right information': his familiarity with the social context which is absent from the observation notes but which can be provided by the researcher's own experience of the event.

Expressing the relationship between the documentary record and the unofficial record in sociolinguistic terms helps to forge an image of analysis in classroom research as an active and creative process involving the re-construction of meaning by the researcher as he re-works the data in the light of his experience. Rob Walker writes that:

> the task of research is to make sense of what we know. The investigator dismantles and reassembles conventional or common-sense meanings, altering the balance between what seems strange and what seems familiar, striving to find new ways of looking at the world (1980, p. 224).
> . . . Significance has to be won from the chaotic patterns: 'meaning' does not naturally fall out of the data, sense has to be made of it (1980, p. 234).

As soon as the documentary record in case-study research is seen as potentially-meaningful language, rather than merely as facts, the unofficial record becomes an indispensable component of the data, and the analysis of that record perforce becomes a personal interpretive activity. And because this method of analysis is explicitly interpretive it is in a real sense far less of a 'fiction' than traditional quantitative research methods which 'give no clues as to the actual process of discovery, to the ways conventional wisdom has had to be stretched and squeezed' (Walker, 1980, p. 228).

Research as reading
Anyone familiar with the writings of psycholinguists on the subject of children's reading will react to all this talk of 'sensible guesses' and 'context', of 'constructing meaning' and 'making sense', with a strong sense of *déjà vu*. We've heard this before somewhere. Consider Margaret Meek's description of the act of reading, bearing in mind what I have suggested so far about the process of analysis/interpretation in case-study research:

> In the act of reading what someone has written, we enter into a kind of social relationship with the writer who has something to tell us or something to make with words and language. The reader takes on this relationship, which may feel like listening, but is in

fact different in that it is more active. He recreates the meaning by processing the text at his own speed and in his own way. As he brings the text to life, he casts back and forth in his head for connections between what he is reading and what he already knows. His eyes scan forward or jump backwards. He pauses, rushes on, selects from his memory whatever relates the meaning to his experience or his earlier reading, in a rich and complex system of to-ing and fro-ing in his head, storing, reworking, understanding or being puzzled. Some successful readers say that they feel they are helping to create the work *with* the author. (1982, pp. 20-1)

This eloquent account of the reading act, which celebrates the active, personal and interpretive response to a text by a reader, can clearly be read as an extended metaphor of the act of analysis in case-study research. This is not entirely a coincidence, since both psycholinguistics and case-study research share an emphasis on the *meaning* which individuals make of their experience, and a rejection of mechanistic views of social action. In this sense both disciplines are broadly phenemenological in their theoretical orientation.

So, what can the case-study researcher learn from the psycholinguistic view of reading? The insight into the research process provided by sociolinguistics, which helped to support a view of data as text, and of analysis as active contextualization, can now be further extended by psycholinguistics by suggesting that the interplay between the documentary record and the researcher's experience approximates a 'reading' of the data. And the 'meaning' of the researcher's data is no more intrinsic to the words of the tape transcript than the 'meaning' of a reader's text is intrinsic to the words on the page. Whatever 'meaning' there is in the transcript is the product of an interaction between the words and the researcher's inside knowledge, or as I.A. Richards puts it (1943, p.94):

... the proper meaning of a passage (what it really means) is a kind of scholastic ghost with very much less in it than a good reader will rightly find there.

Reading as research

The analogy is not one-way, however. Formulations of the reading act may shed light on the task of analysis in research, but at the same time much can be learned about the task of reading from descriptions of the research process. Although psycholinguistics supports a vision of research analysis as an active, personal and interpretive response to the data by a researcher, recall that this was only part of the solution to the problematic relationship between the documentary record and the unofficial record. There was a significant sociolinguistic element to the picture as well. For Halliday a text is not merely part of a specific communication between individual speakers and hearers (or, for the reading act, writers and readers). Text is also located within a complex network of social structures and relationships – the semiotic system.

Text – whether it be a researcher's tape transcripts and observation notes, or a child's book — is produced within an elaborate social context which is 'entered into' and 'recreated' by the researcher/analyst or by the child/reader when the text is received. But at the same time, written text of any kind is *received* within an elaborate social context which is almost certainly different from the situation within which the text was *produced*. This receiving-end context is, too, an integral part of the interaction between written text and reading situation. The researcher 'receives' the text of his own documentary record within a social context quite unlike the social context within which he 'produced' it. The classroom where the data were collected differs markedly from the academic environment in which the analysis is carried out, but both contexts will influence the sense he makes of the data. Similarly, for a child in school, the social context in which he or she 'receives' the text of a book probably bears no relation to the social context from which the text came. The act of reading a text in the classroom is, for a child, inextricably bound up with the social structures and relationships operating there, and the sense he or she makes of the text will be influenced by that context at least as much as by the context in which the text was produced. Angela Hale has observed that 'what counts as reading varies according to the demands of the social situation' (1980, p. 25) and that, in school, this social situation embraces relationships between teachers and pupils, definitions of reading and literacy, and structures of knowledge and power, which will combine to shape the meaning of reading acts (Hale, 1979 and 1980). How, for example, can we separate Colin's 'reading' of the text on Brasilia either from the immediate classroom business surrounding the interaction between Colin and Ms Harvey or from the structural significance which the event of reading aloud has for both Colin and his teacher?

Psycholinguists point to the importance of the 'kind of social relationship with the writer' which the reader 'enters into' as he or she engaged with the text. Sociolinguists, on the other hand, can provide the basis for a more structural description of the task of reading at school, which involves the entering into a social relationship of a very different kind — the more immediate interaction with teachers and peers in a classroom context. This is what the research can tell us about children's reading, even though that part of the research from which the message arises is its process rather than its findings. A reading of a text, whether by a researcher or pupil, is a social and cultural activity, and as such it will be affected by and in turn have its own influence upon the social structures and relationships within which that reading of the text takes place.

Assessment as sense-making

What then can be learned from this about the classroom teacher faced with the task of evaluating pupils' reading? My argument so far, that the act of research analysis and the act of reading are analogous *kinds* of tasks, applies equally to classroom reading assessment. Coming to 'know' a reader is, after all, a case of making meaning within a complex social context. Just as for research and reading, a sociolinguistic emphasis makes explicit two vital aspects of reading assessment. First, it reinforces the sense-making nature of assessment, in contrast with the widely-held belief that it is an unambiguous mechanical operation. Second, it locates the assessment process within (to use Halliday's term once again) a 'situation' which comprises a complex network of social structures and relationships.

And yet, however much a sociolinguistic perspective may facilitate research analysis by legitimizing the 'unofficial' dimension of the researcher's data, it also magnifies the central methodological difficulty in 'making sense' of teachers' reading assessment practices in the classroom. I began by recognizing that the reading assessment taking place between Colin and his teacher seemed so embedded in the fabric of meaning in the classroom that it was difficult to tease out its particular significance. Despite the insights about that scene afforded by the inclusion of the 'black market record', this central problem of 'embeddedness' is not greatly overcome. In what sense can we say that Ms Harvey is *assessing* Colin's reading, on the basis of (official as well as unofficial) evidence available to us?

Does the scene's significance for reading assessment derive from the information about Colin as a reader, which is 'available' to Ms Harvey in Colin's oral reading? Does it derive from the fact that Colin's 'promotion', to the next reading book in the scheme, was 'at stake' here? Does it derive from the fact that Colin was ultimately allowed to exchange his reading book for the 'next one up' in the reading scheme? Does it derive from the possibility that Ms Harvey may draw on her perceptions about Colin's reading during this episode when later required to communicate her appraisal of Colin as a reader to parents, other teachers, and so on? Does it derive from the fact that Ms Harvey has reported in interview that she bases her judgements of children's reading on their oral reading fluency? Or does it derive from the extent to which Colin and Ms Harvey *behave* as though Colin's reading is being assessed? It all depends on our definition of 'reading assessment', a term which is generally taken to stand for practices with a self-evident existence but which for a researcher are very difficult to identify and describe. If the classroom observer defines 'reading assessment' as *the formation of judgements, by teachers, about children with respect to their competence as readers,* he is attempting to identify a process which is by definition hidden (i.e. inside the teacher's head) and therefore unavailable for inspection. He can describe the *sources* from which information about children's reading may have been gathered ('texts'). He can describe the *settings* within which that information was available ('situations'). And he can describe words and actions which appear to be the *outcomes* of reading assessment. He cannot, however, infer from either the sources and settings, or the outcomes, that the *process* of reading assessment has necessarily taken place. So long as he defines reading assessment as a judgement-making process rather than an observable form of behaviour, the nearest he can get is by carefully describing *all* possible manifestations of reading assessment, and by building up a picture which is the composite of these varied and sometimes contradictory representations.

Of course, gaining access to hidden processes is not a problem which only concerns students of classroom reading assessment. The reading process itself is widely held to be a hidden process (i.e. it happens inside the reader's head) and is therefore unavailable for inspection. Differing definitions of reading have generated differing approaches to gaining access to it, but these approaches invariably render (private) reading public by means of a product or outcome of reading. If reading really is a hidden process then these products and outcomes are only 'the visible tip of far less accessible behaviour' (Pugh, 1978, p. 89), in which case close attention to those aspects of reading which are closest to the reader, i.e. the 'text' and 'situation' of a reading act, are probably more reliable indicators of the quality of a reader's experience. Building up a picture of readers based on all possible manifestations of reading, whether they corroborate each other or not, is probably the nearest we can get. This is what Margaret Spencer calls for when she writes that 'we should do well to move our feet and eyes and try to see what the learning looks like from where the learner stands, his book in hand' (1980, p. 61). Teachers often have his kind of intuitive sense of how their pupils experience reading. If assessment is a sense-making, rather than a technical, exercise, this 'black market record' will form an indispensable context against which other, more outcome-based, assessments will be made sense of. Recovering the process by which that 'unofficial record' is produced may be an impossible research task, but its existence and legitimacy should not be questioned.

Conclusion

By exploring the parallels between case-study research, children's reading and teachers' assessment practices, I have tried to demonstrate the general point that new insights can be gained by examining the relationship between the processes under investigation in educational research, and the process of discovery and sense-making within the research itself. It is a principle which I have only begun to develop here, but which I think deserves further analysis. Rob Walker writes that 'the subject being studied can impose its own authority on the sense that is made of it by the investigator' (1980, p. 224). In the present project the subjects being studied did more than impose their own authority on the sense I made of them: they provided living examples of sense-making activities which reinforced the foundation for an interpretive methodology. By the same token an approach to research, which made explicit its dependence on social interaction and relationships for access to the meaning of classroom events, helped to highlight the inseparability of children's reading, or teachers' assessment practices, from the context of background knowledge and social interaction through which they occur. For me, the recognition that the teacher assessing reading, the child reading a text, and myself studying teachers' practices, were all in a real sense engaged in analogous kinds of sense-making activities, sharpened my understanding of all three tasks.

Notes

1. Pseudonyms are used throughout for persons' names.
2. The following notation is used in the transcription of Colin's reading:

/ /	indicates pause;
(*miscues* 'inland')	indicates that the word preceding the brackets is a miscue of the word in brackets;
(*self-corrects*)	indicates that pupil corrects own miscue without audible prompt;
'of-of'	indicates repetition;
(*inserts* 'see')	indicates that word in brackets was vocalized by pupil but does not appear in text.

The text Colin reads in the transcript is pp. 119-20 of FLOWERDEW, P. (1972), *New Interest: Book Two*. Edinburgh: Oliver and Boyd.

References

EDWARDS, A.D. and FURLONG, V.J. (1978), *The Language of Teaching*. London: Heinemann Educational Books.

GIDDENS, A. (1976), *New Rules of Sociological Method*. London: Hutchinson.

HALE, A. (1979), 'Hearing children read: a sociological analysis of the definition of reading implicit in a routine teaching activity.' Unpublished Ph.D. thesis, University of Manchester.

────── (1980), 'The social relationships implicit in approaches to reading.' *Reading*, 14, 1, July.

HALLIDAY, M.A.K. (1976), *Learning How to Mean*. London: Edward Arnold.

────── (1978), *Language as Social Semiotic*. London: Edward Arnold.

HOLLAND, N.N. (1975), *Five Readers Reading*. London: Routledge and Kegan Paul.

HULL, C. (1981), 'Between the lines: data analysis as an exact art.' Paper presented to the 1981 conference of the British Educational Research Association.

MEEK, M. (1982), *Learning to Read.* London: The Bodley Head.

PUGH, A.K. (1978), *Silent Reading: An introduction to its study and teaching.* London: Heinemann Educational Books.

RICHARDS, I.A. (1943), *How to Read a Page.* London: Routledge and Kegan Paul.

SPENCER, M. (1980), 'Handing down the magic.' in Salmon, P. (ed.), *Coming to Know.* London: Routledge and Kegan Paul.

WALKER, R. (1980) 'Making sense and losing meaning: problems of selection in doing case study,' in Simons, H. (ed.), *Towards a Science of the Singular: Essays about case-study research and evaluation.* Norwich: Centre for Applied Research in Education, University of East Anglia.

WILLIS, P. (1976) 'The man in the iron cage: notes on method.' *Working Papers in Cultural Studies.* Centre for Contemporary Cultural Studies, University of Birmingham, pp.135-43.